KISISI (OUR LANGUAGE)

New Directions in Ethnography is a series of contemporary, original works. Each title has been selected and developed to meet the needs of readers seeking finely grained ethnographies that treat key areas of anthropological study. What sets these books apart from other ethnographies is their form and style. They have been written with care to allow both specialists and nonspecialists to delve into theoretically sophisticated work. This objective is achieved by structuring each book so that one portion of the text is ethnographic narrative while another portion unpacks the theoretical arguments and offers some basic intellectual genealogy for the theories underpinning the work.

Each volume in *New Directions in Ethnography* aims to immerse readers in fundamental anthropological ideas, as well as to illuminate and engage more advanced concepts. Inasmuch, these volumes are designed to serve not only as scholarly texts, but also as teaching tools and as vibrant, innovative ethnographies that showcase some of the best that contemporary anthropology has to offer.

Published volumes

1. *Turf Wars: Discourse, Diversity, and the Politics of Place*
By Gabriella Gahlia Modan

2. *Homegirls: Language and Cultural Practice among Latina Youth Gangs*
By Norma Mendoza-Denton

3. *Allah Made Us: Sexual Outlaws in an Islamic African City*
By Rudolf Pell Gaudio

4. *Political Oratory and Cartooning: An Ethnography of Democratic Processes in Madagascar*
By Jennifer Jackson

5. *Transcultural Teens: Performing Youth Identities in French Cités*
By Chantal Tetreault

6. *Kisisi (Our Language): The Story of Colin and Sadiki*
By Perry Gilmore

KISISI (OUR LANGUAGE)

The Story of Colin and Sadiki

Perry Gilmore

WILEY Blackwell

This edition first published 2016
© 2016 Perry Gilmore

Registered Office
John Wiley & Sons Ltd, The Atrium, Southern Gate, Chichester, West Sussex, PO19 8SQ, UK

Editorial Offices
350 Main Street, Malden, MA 02148-5020, USA
9600 Garsington Road, Oxford, OX4 2DQ, UK
The Atrium, Southern Gate, Chichester, West Sussex, PO19 8SQ, UK

For details of our global editorial offices, for customer services, and for information about how to apply for permission to reuse the copyright material in this book please see our website at www.wiley.com/wiley-blackwell.

The right of Perry Gilmore to be identified as the author of this work has been asserted in accordance with the UK Copyright, Designs and Patents Act 1988.

Library of Congress Cataloging-in-Publication Data

Gilmore, Perry.
   Kisisi (our language) : the story of Colin and Sadiki / Perry Gilmore.
      pages cm. – (New directions in ethnography ; 6)
   Includes bibliographical references and index.
   ISBN 978-1-119-10156-7 (cloth) – ISBN 978-1-119-10157-4 (pbk.)   1. Languages, Mixed–Kenya.   2. Languages in contact–Kenya.   3. Children–Language.   I. Title.   II. Series: New directions in ethnography ; 6.
   PM7802.G55 2015
   417.22096762–dc23
                              2015012853

A catalogue record for this book is available from the British Library.

Cover image: Photograph taken by Perry Gilmore at the Gilgil Baboon Research Project Headquarters on Kekopey Ranch near Gilgil, Kenya in 1975.

Set in 11/13pt Bembo by Aptara Inc., New Delhi, India

1   2016

This book is dedicated to my son, Colin Gilmore,
and my husband David Smith.
I am inspired by and long for you both
every day.

CONTENTS

ACKNOWLEDGMENTS

This book has been four decades in the making and has benefited from myriad conversations with friends, family, colleagues, and students who have helped shape my thinking and encouraged my efforts. I am deeply indebted to them all. My late husband, David Smith, was my strongest and most enthusiastic supporter. His research on language dialect, variation, and change inspired my own study. Reading his articles on pidgin and creole languages before I went to Kenya introduced me to the study of language contact phenomena and their potential comparisons with child language development. This background knowledge, along with my own professional interest in child language studies, contributed to my heightened awareness of the compelling significance of Colin and Sadiki's creative language invention and prompted me to document and record their everyday talk and social interactions.

I owe special thanks to colleagues and friends including Ray McDermott, Shelley Goldman, Michelle Fine, Norma Mendoza-Denton, Bambi Schieffelin, Terri McCarty, Susan Philips, Penny Eckert, Janet Theophano, Deborah Tannen, Aomar Boum, Sarah Engel, Elena Houle, Robi Craig Erickson, Concha Delgado-Gaitan, Jody Gilmore, Juliet Gilmore-Larkin, Beth Leonard, Luis Moll, Lisa Delpit, Nancy Hornberger, Jane Hill, Courtney Cazden, and Shirley Brice Heath. They have all offered much appreciated support, critical feedback, and ongoing dialogue about this very personal research project. This book has benefited from their knowledge, wisdom, interest, and encouragement. Others who also strongly influenced my research while I was at the University of Pennsylvania included Dell Hymes, Bill Labov, Gillian Sankoff, Erving Goffman, and Lila Gleitman.

I was fortunate to have my former doctoral student, Heidi Orcutt-Kachiri, review and edit an earlier draft of this book. Heidi's fieldwork in Kenya, fluency in Swahili, and editorial expertise and generosity made her an invaluable resource. Much appreciation also goes to my graduate student, Susanna Schippers, who proof read an earlier version of the draft manuscript. I am grateful to many students who have participated in my classes in language acquisition, discourse analysis, applied linguistics and the anthropology of childhood. They have raised important questions and provided critical insights about this study over the years. Special appreciation goes to my graduate assistants Satoko Seigel, Shri Ramakrishnan, Lauren Zentz, Katie Silvester, and Paola Delgado.

Colleagues, friends, and family who shared time with me in Kenya were kind enough to read and respond to earlier drafts of this book. I thank Colin's father, Hugh Gilmore, who also helped me record the language data, Shirley Strum, Bob Harding, Andrew Hill, and Barbara Terry. Their critical comments and questions helped affirm memories and further problematize the challenging circumstances of the complex social world we all experienced in postcolonial Kenya. Janet McIntosh also provided more current perspectives based on her recent research on postcolonial settler life in Kenya.

In 2009, my colleague, Peggy Miller, recalling my first publication on the boys' language in 1979, invited me to write about the research anew for an interdisciplinary encyclopedia, *The Child,* that she was co-editing with Richard Shweder for the University of Chicago Press. I was struck that after more than 30 years Peggy remembered the research so vividly and considered it relevant today. Coincidently, just a few months later, Mikael Parkvall, a Swedish linguist and a pidgin scholar whom I hadn't known, contacted me after discovering the same 1979 article online. Both Mikael's and Peggy's interest in and enthusiasm about the work, after so many years, inspired me to finally reopen the dusty boxes of data that were filled with recordings, films, photos, letters, and journals that I had collected decades before. I am deeply indebted to them both for motivating me and taking the work so seriously. They reminded me of the important responsibility I had to reframe and share this study. Mikael Parkvall additionally provided lengthy and detailed feedback on an earlier draft of this book. His linguistic expertise and generosity were deeply appreciated.

The editorial team at Wiley-Blackwell has been extremely encouraging and has provided a perfect home for the book in the *New Directions in Ethnography* series. I especially thank Elizabeth Swayze, Wiley-Blackwell's Commissioning Editor, for her strong enthusiasm and persuasive belief in this work. Mary Hall, Editorial Assistant, and Ben Thatcher, Project Editor, have graciously helped make the production phase of publication go smoothly. The series editors, Norma Mendoza-Denton and Galey

Modan, provided deeply appreciated professional enthusiasm, astute editorial insights and much of their valuable time.

A writing grant from the Southwest Educational Development Laboratory supported the preparation of my 1979 article on this topic published in *Working Papers in Sociolinguistics*. Portions of the data presented in this book originally appeared in that article. An earlier analysis of some of the data also appeared in an article published in the *Anthropology and Education Quarterly* in 2011 in a special issue edited by Nancy Hornberger honoring the work of Dell Hymes. A sabbatical leave from the University of Arizona, College of Education in 2013–2014 provided the opportunity to write the book. A brief retreat in a serene Vermont setting, generously hosted by my friends Robby Mohatt, Justin Mohatt, and Jim Cummings, provided a special space to complete final editorial revisions.

I want to thank my family – Susan Raefsky, Elena, Gary, and Lana Houle, Jodi Smith and Hansil Stokes, Cindy and Tom Ryan, Jesse, Seth and Cameron Meyer, Tommy and Michael Ryan, and Jamie Smith. They have always been a steady support for me and I dearly love and appreciate them all. Aomar Boum, Norma Mendoza-Denton, and Maggie Boum, who are like family to me, were especially supportive while I was writing the book. Also part of my extended family support network here in Tucson are Velma and Bob Rutman on whom I depend for so much. We are all further connected to our African family through Sadiki Elim, my son Colin's cherished childhood friend. Though I have not been back to Kenya since I left in 1976, we have managed to remain closely bonded. There have been many long skype calls with Sadiki, his parents, wife, children, and other family members, including Timothy Leperes Laur and David Laur. The family's complete pleasure and pride in the project have further inspired me to complete the book.

Finally, I am profoundly grateful to two beautiful five-year-old boys, Colin Gilmore and Sadiki Elim, who loved each other unabashedly on an Up-Country Kenya hillside and expressed that love in a language that helped them face the challenges of postcolonial racism that dominated their lives. I am honored and privileged to share their sweet story. It is my hope that the boys will amaze you today as they did me so long ago. Sadiki and Colin's story urges us to look more closely and see all children with a little more awe, wonder, and respect.

MAP

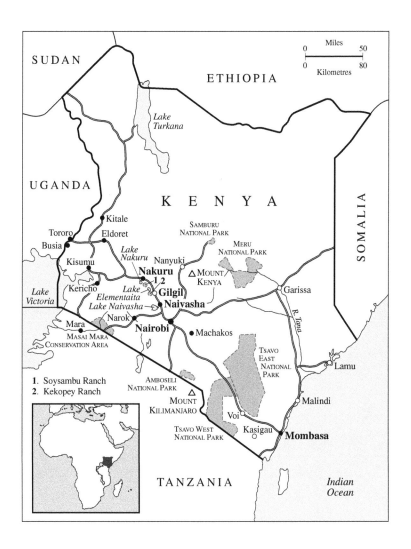

PROLOGUE

Like the Ancient Mariner in Samuel Coleridge's classic poem, I have a story to tell. In Coleridge's *Rime of the Ancient Mariner,* the old man stops the wedding guest, and with his hypnotic "glittering eye" begins his compelling narration with the words, "There was a ship." He tells the captivated listener about powerful life and death events that occurred many years before. He tells his tale to leave the listener sadder and wiser from this lesson in humanity but also to find some healing for his own long-held pain. My own story, like the Mariner's, is a deeply felt personal life story that tells of events that took place many years ago. My own narrative might begin with the words, "There was a boy."

Indeed, there was a boy. It has been a quarter of a century since my sweet son died. Colin Gilmore was killed by a drunk driver when he was only 18. Unusually loving and easily loved, Colin drew people to him like a charmed magnet. Born with what seemed like an uncanny sense of social justice, he fearlessly embraced what he felt was right and good, and passionately confronted what he felt wasn't. Colin left a huge and gaping hole in this world and in my heart. He has also left an important story for me to tell. Like the Ancient Mariner, I am compelled to tell and retell his story with the hope that there may be lessons learned and wisdom gained from the life events my son led me to witness. Like the Ancient Mariner, the telling also helps to heal my pain.

The tale I tell begins four decades ago, when Colin was five. It is a story about two little boys – their friendship and their creative language invention. By chance, Colin met Sadiki, a handsome five-year-old Samburu boy, when they became neighbors and friends for 15 months on a remote and isolated multilingual Kenya hillside. A little more than a decade after British rule ended in 1963, their postcolonial encounter at the complex borders of language and culture grew into a close, and often controversial, friendship that was created through, and marked by, their invention of a special private language, a Swahili pidgin (a simplified variety of Swahili) that was understood and shared only by the two of them.

Part historic ethnography, part linguistic case study, and part a bereaved mother's memoir, the mixed genre narrative and multidisciplinary discussion that follow offer a brief glimpse into Colin and Sadiki's world – a love story about two five-year-old boys who simultaneously created a special bond and a special language – both inextricably woven together. The narrative seeks to blend scholarship and personal memory in order to evocatively describe their close border-crossing friendship and their innovative private language – its structure, uses, and meanings, and the creative processes of negotiation and collaborative invention they drew on to generate it. The story also explores the ways in which their invented language helped them construct new identities and resist, transgress, and transform the marked postcolonial borders and harsh inequities of economics, race, and culture that engulfed them and dominated the social power relationships and language ideologies that engaged all aspects of their daily lives.

Today, Sadiki is a hard-working accomplished man in his forties with a family and young children of his own. He remembers his close friendship with Colin more than he remembers the details of the language they created. I have become the lone keeper of their language. The boys' special friendship left a significant gift – a rare language legacy that contributes to our understanding of how young children's linguistic creativity and agentive power enabled them to invent a new language and interrupt the oppressive hegemonic colonial social and symbolic order around them through their everyday playful and loving verbal interactions. The story of their language invention provides insight into the nature of language – its origins, maintenance, change, and loss. Their story documents a close examination of children's astounding creative expressive abilities, too often unrecognized and drastically underestimated in the research literature and in educational policies and practices.

Years ago when the boys were still young, I wrote several academic papers describing various aspects of their language. At that time and with the encouragement of scholars in the field, I had planned to continue my analysis and to later develop the individual papers into a manuscript that could tell their story more holistically, from beginning to end. But for many years after Colin's death, I could not touch or talk about these data. As the years have passed, I have felt a pressing responsibility to revisit these events. I have been compelled to describe in more detail the boys' everyday life experiences and their creative language invention.

I share Colin and Sadiki's story now in honor and celebration of Colin's memory and of the unique bond of language and love these two beautiful boys shared for a brief period of their lives more than 40 years ago. I also share their story in celebration of *all* children and their brilliance as innovative language users, keenly observant cultural critics, and strong social activists. I share their story, finally, because I know of no other quite like it. Many other children, to varying degrees, have had similar experiences, especially in diverse multilingual settings and contact zones where transformative energy and linguistic and cultural resources are abundant and available for the creation of new verbal expressive forms. However, only minimally descriptive and anecdotal reports of similar or related language phenomena exist in the literature.

By an unplanned set of circumstances, I found myself in a position to recognize, observe, and document Sadiki and Colin's innovative dynamic language experiences as they unfolded. I recount these serendipitous events as I have lived and witnessed them, hoping the reader will share my awe and wonder at the children's creative language virtuosity and the innocent yet powerful sense of love, loyal friendship, and social justice that is tightly woven into the very fabric of their daily language practices.

Their story seems simple and small, yet it raises profound questions and has direct implications for many fields of study including anthropology, psychology, education, and linguistics. While this unanticipated study was stimulated by and focuses on the boys' unique and spontaneous invented language, the narrative that follows will highlight aspects of the boys' daily lived experiences and the social worlds and linguistic ecologies[1] they regularly navigated. Rather than focus exclusively on the detailed descriptions and analysis of the structure and form of their private language in a vacuum, the narrative that follows embeds the discussion of their language in the multilayered historical, sociopolitical and cultural contexts that gave meaning to it and in the everyday lives and language practices of the children who created it.

The first chapter describes a personal account of the serendipitous discovery of their language in the context of their hillside encounter and newly found friendship. The second explores their language in relationship to historical, age-old questions about the origins of language, language genesis studies, and the emergence of other "new" languages and language varieties. The third chapter examines their language experiences aesthetically with a focus on the significance of play, creativity, performance, and verbal art in language invention. Chapter 4 ethnographically illuminates the colonial and postcolonial social structures that dominated and dramatically affected the children's lives, their friendship, and their language practices.

Chapter 5 focuses on the children's language, describing its form and structure and analyzing the dynamic discursive processes they negotiated to invent and continuously expand their new language.

Aware that parts of the narrative may be too evocative for the linguist or too linguistic and technical for the nonlinguist, too academic for the parent, and too nonacademic for the scholar, I have attempted to speak from a position that seeks to maintain both the humanity and authenticity of the children's story and the academic veracity and ethical integrity of the scientific scholarly inquiry. I have tried to make each aspect of the telling accessible to the nonspecialist and general reader. I encourage the reader to stay with the unfolding multidisciplinary narrative in all its various interwoven forms and voices, from the descriptive personal accounts, the political histories and ethnographic details, to the more structured linguistic analysis. Each of these different aspects of their many-sided story helps to contextualize, enrich, and illuminate significant facets of the little polished gem that they have left us. Each lens – the personal, historical, aesthetic, ethnographic, and linguistic – reveals distinct and meaningful dimensions of their experience as friends, as playmates, as language creators, and as courageous social activists. Each perspective contributes to a fuller understanding of their unusual story.

In what Johannes Fabian[2] might describe as a "late ethnography," that (re)presents and interprets "historically situated events and practices," I write this account in 2015, 40 years after I experienced it. I have therefore tried to produce a multivocal narrative relying on a range of others' voices from scholarly sources, colonial memoirs, historical nonfiction, film, and social media to enrich and complicate my own limited experiences, interpretations, and memories. I especially draw on direct accounts of others describing relevant historical individuals, events, and political circumstances, narrating these events from a personal storytelling position as Colin's mother. With all the biases that both limit and enrich my understandings, I attempt to bring the reader more intimately into my own and the children's experiences, and into the liminal spaces they explored at the marginal threshold of their imaginative and artful language creativity and their transgressive border-crossing friendship.

The story of Colin and Sadiki presents a brief portrait of their friendship and the ephemeral language they created to sustain it. The examination of the linguistic and semiotic processes they enlisted to navigate and transcend those borders enriches our understanding of language and culture by providing a concrete and processual example of child language invention – a close and intimate look at their language-in-the-making. What follows is a human story of irrepressible expressive creativity and the politics of language and oppression. It is an ethnographic exploration of young children's critical and resilient discursive agency in their innocent yet effective quest for language equality and a place for their friendship on the rigid borders of their vastly different language and cultural worlds.

CHAPTER 1

UWERYUMACHINI!: A LANGUAGE DISCOVERED

The limits of language are reached when language becomes unfamiliar, alien, altered. The limits mark a boundary between the known and the unknown, between the self and the other ... The confrontation with the unknown in language inevitably produces a reassessment of the known. Stories of the encounter with the other have written into them stories of the discovery, and rediscovery, of the self.

Martin Calder[1]

"serendipity" ... the discovery, by chance or sagacity, of valid results which were not sought for ... the observation is anomalous, surprising, either because it seems inconsistent with prevailing theory or with other established facts. In either case, the seeming inconsistency provokes curiosity; it stimulates the investigator to "make sense of the datum," to fit it into a broader framework of knowledge.

Robert Merton[2]

"Uweryumachini!!" Colin and Sadiki kicked up puffs of hot pale dust as they jumped up and down, excitedly yelling and pointing to a small airplane flying high above them in the clear blue Kenya sky. "Uweryumachini!" They gleefully giggled and shouted. With outstretched arms they reached up, jumping high, as if to touch the winged visitor. Then turning to each other, face to face, with their mouths and eyes wide open in exaggerated

Kisisi (Our Language): The Story of Colin and Sadiki, First Edition. Perry Gilmore
© 2016 Perry Gilmore. Published 2016 by John Wiley & Sons, Inc.

expressions of surprise, they burst into wild laughter again. Huge smiles flashed across their faces as they loudly chanted over and over, "Uweryumachini!!" Eyes glistening with delight, they continued their ecstatic shouting and jumping with eager rhythmic repetition. It was as if the greatest discovery had just interrupted their daily morning soccer ball ritual. The unexpected airborne surprise buzzed its way across the vast sky that reflected itself perfectly in the flamingo-rimmed glassy blue soda lake below. It buzzed high over the endless savannah landscape marked by dramatic volcanic craters and the sharply carved lines of precipitous steep scarps and rocky cliffs that were so characteristic of this part of the Great Rift Valley. The massive sky and uninterrupted sweeping panoramic view surrounded the two little boys in all directions. "Uweryumachini!! Uweryumachini!!" Their voices rang out on the remote hillside wrapped in playful giggles as they shared their sheer, intense, and playful joy!

It was 1975. Colin's father and I were both graduate students studying the communicative behaviors of a troop of 92 wild olive baboons (*Papio anubis*). Hugh Gilmore, my husband then, was a doctoral student in physical anthropology at the University of Pennsylvania, conducting his dissertation research on adult male face-to-face social interaction with a focus on their communicative vocalizations. I was completing research for my Master's degree in education, focused on developmental psychology at Temple University, examining how juvenile baboons learned, interpreted, and displayed their place in, and knowledge of, the troop's complex hierarchical ranking system.[3] We were observing a free-ranging baboon troop that previous researchers had named the Pumphouse Gang, after the Tom Wolfe book.[4] The aptly named baboon troop often "hung out" near a small pump house, a pumping station for the ranch's water supply system that was at the bottom of a cliff in the center of their home range. The Pumphouse Gang was one of many troops that lived and foraged on Kekopey Ranch, a sprawling 48,000 acre cattle farm near the town of Gilgil, Kenya. Arthur and Tobina Cole, the ranch's aristocratic British colonial second-generation Kenya land owners, had generously made an old uninhabited manager's house available as a headquarters for the Gilgil Baboon Research Project.

For the five years before we arrived, the headquarters had been home to a string of primatologists, mostly students of the American physical anthropologist Sherwood Washburn, a pioneer in the field of primatology. The house was situated on an isolated hillside on a high bluff at the far south end of the huge ranch, eight miles from the Coles' antique-filled historic farmhouse. The baboon headquarters was an airy six-room tin-roofed stone bungalow with the exterior painted a deep earth-colored red. The Red

House (*Kiserigwa*), as it was often called, would be our family's new home for the next 15 months.

The researchers at the Gilgil Baboon Research Project shared the hillside with a half dozen African ranch workers and their families. The African workers' way of life stood in striking contrast to both the aristocratic entitled lifestyle of the British colonial land owners and to the privileged position of the Gilgil Baboon Project's researchers. The hillside African residents worked either for the ranch or for the project earning very meager wages. The Gilgil Baboon Project workers were better paid, earning increasing amounts over the years, from $40 a month in the early years, up to $100 in the later years. They lived with their families in two very small one-room stone dwellings just over the rise, about 50 yards away, on the other side of the hill. Sadiki was the son of a Samburu mother and Turkana father. Sadiki's parents were ranch workers for the Coles. Sadiki and his four sisters lived in one of the stone dwellings on the hillside with their parents, who herded cattle on foot and ran the pumps for the cattle's water supply, fed from a hot spring on the far north side of the ranch.

The cluster of African families on the hillside was multilingual, representing four to six tribal peoples. Each family spoke its own tribal language to each other. There was a broad range of diverse linguistic repertoires including Abaluhya, also known as Luhya, a Bantu language, and Luo, Maasai, Turkana, and Samburu (i.e., North Maa), all Nilotic languages with Luo being more distantly related to the others. There was occasional use of Kipsigis, Boran, and Somali depending on the presence of rotating ranch employees living on the hill. Our family spoke English as had all the previous researchers in the Red House. The language used to communicate across these highly marked and compartmentalized linguistic and cultural borders was a regional variety of Kiswahili, often called Up-Country Swahili, Kitchen Swahili, Kisetta, or Kisettla.[5] The local variety of Swahili spoken in this region of the Kenya bush is not to be confused with Standard or East Coast Kiswahili.[6] This Up-Country variety, a simplified or pidginized Swahili that Hancock has referred to as the "most aberrant variety"[7] of Swahili, was a second language for African people living in Up-Country Kenya. It was also historically the language the colonial employers used to communicate with their African servants and workers.

The first day we arrived at the headquarters, all of the hillside residents were lined up in the small open courtyard standing in a row ready to formally greet the new *wazungu* (white) researchers. They had heard us approaching long before we turned our white Kombi Volkswagen bus on to the long dirt track that led up the hill to the Red House. Mike and Cordelia Rose, colleagues who were studying colobus monkeys at nearby Lake Naivasha, had kindly hosted us in their small whitewashed mud and wattle thatched roof cottage the night before. The distinctive bellows, snorts, and grunts of nearby hippos and myriad other strange new animal sounds filled the cool night air as our little family tried to fall asleep anticipating the new life awaiting us, just miles away.

In the morning Mike and Cordelia led us, caravan style, to the headquarters where they had often visited the previous baboon researchers. Our two vehicles stirred up long trailing veils of tawny dust clouds as we made our way across the parched and sun-baked savannah and up the hill, stopping to carefully open and close the cattle paddock gates before arriving at the headquarters. We all climbed out of the vehicles and began to exchange *jambo*'s (hello's), smiles and introductions, each of us shaking hands as we walked down the warm and welcoming reception line.

Colin and Sadiki's eyes fixed on each other almost immediately. Sadiki stood out among his older and younger sisters. The boys were just about the same height and age. We would discover later that their birthdays were only one month apart. In the midst of the initial awkward formality and confusion around our introductions, everyone easily observed the instant magnetism between the two boys. Their new friendship took only a few days to emerge. From the fourth day after we arrived at the research station, Sadiki and Colin spent most of their days together, sunrise to sunset. They were to become inseparable friends, playing together almost daily for the next 15 months.

Initially the two children struggled to communicate in the local Up-Country Swahili, visibly using lots of gestures and charades during the first days and weeks. A soccer ball, a wheel rim and a stick, an old rope swing hanging from the lone tree in the courtyard, and the collection of match box cars Colin brought with him were favorite and frequent play props. Lying side by side on Colin's bed, looking at *Tintin* comic books, they softly pointed out pictures of *simba* (lion), *samaki* (fish), and the few Swahili words they seemed to know in common. It was heartwarming to observe them together. A little more than a month after our arrival, I wrote in my journal, "Sitting on the little wooden kitchen chairs in the cool courtyard shade, Sadiki patiently teaches Colin a melodious traditional Samburu song. Sadiki's rich peaceful voice sounds so wise and old for just a little boy as he softly chants the haunting Samburu melody; trance-like, tranquil, and knowing. Colin hums along catching a few syllables and soon his little voice is singing along and sounding surprisingly deep and wise and peaceful too." Within just a few months they seemed to be in effortless and continual conversation as they pretended to hunt herds of Thomson gazelles in the tall grasses or raced match box cars in an imaginary African safari rally game, each playing "Action Man" or "Batman."

I was treasuring their budding friendship and so pleased to see Colin learning Swahili in such a playful loving way. He had not really been all that enthusiastic about the more formal vocabulary instruction I had been offering. In those early weeks I hadn't yet realized that Sadiki's first and primary language in the home was actually Samburu and that he was not a fluent Swahili speaker.

"Uweryumachini! Uweryumachini!" The two boys called out again and again as they continued jumping up and down, pointing to the sky and gleefully shouting at the small airplane flying high above them. Their giggles punctuated each utterance. Their voices carried over the swirl of late morning breezes and through the open window where I was working at my desk. I looked up to see them completely engaged in their exuberant play. I smiled, seeing them enjoying themselves so thoroughly, feeling so glad we had come to Kenya.

"Uweryumachini!" they shouted out again. I strained to listen to what they were saying, their high-pitched laughing voices somewhat muffled by the steady constant breeze so familiar on this high bluff above the basin of the Great Rift Valley. I was certain the local Swahili word for "airplane" was "ndege" but I couldn't quite hear what the boys were calling out. Leafing through my Swahili dictionary, I could find nothing even close to what I thought I heard them shouting. I wasn't sure how to spell or even parse it. Was it a single word? A phrase? I leaned across my desk and called to the boys to come closer to the open window. They approached and I asked them what they were saying. They mumbled something but I still couldn't understand. I urged them to repeat themselves slowly so that I could hear them more clearly. They paused and looked at each other as if a great secret had just been revealed – and not quite sure if they had gotten themselves in trouble. They giggled again, then slowly and hesitantly, with furtive sideways glances at each other, pronounced something that sounded to me like "who-are-you-machini"! They uttered the phrase as a single word with a Swahili "accent." I would eventually discover that their "word" for airplane was part of a continuously expanding vocabulary and grammar that made their speech, a language variety I was to later identify as a spontaneous Swahili pidgin, unintelligible to Swahili speakers.

A little more than two months after our family's arrival to the hillside and within days of my own initial "discovery," it seemed that everyone began to notice that the "Swahili" the boys spoke was "different." While they appeared to speak to each other continuously and to understand each other with ease, no one else could understand them! The Coles and other English visitors to the hillside, hearing the children play, would initially comment on being quite impressed with Colin's fluent Swahili. But after listening for a few more minutes, with a puzzled look, they would remark, "That's *not* Swahili, is it?"

Sadiki's family too had made the discovery. Sadiki's mother explained to us that because the boys loved each other so much, *Mungu* (God) had blessed them with their own special language. This sacred explanation immediately created an unusual close bond between our two families. Sadiki's older "brother" (actually his mother's young brother), David, who stayed with them on his school breaks, offered, "The language they speak is a very complicated one. Nobody understands it but the two of them." News traveled. Visiting relatives, other friends of Sadiki's family, and co-workers on the ranch would come over the rise to the Red House to see, and hear, the boys.

Sadiki's grandfather traveled several hundred miles to visit and to see the *rafiki mzuri* (good friends) that *Mungu* (God) had blessed with this special gift of a "very complicated" language. Our family was summoned to formally meet with him in a clearing on the side of the hill. Unlike most of the ranch workers, who dressed in western clothing, the *mzee* (elder) was dressed traditionally. Holding his long walking staff erect beside him, Sadiki's grandfather stood tall and regal, draped in a loose earth-colored blanket across one shoulder and adorned with traditional earplugs, colorful beaded arm bands, and bracelets. Slowly he began to speak. Both families stood in a circle around him, silent and attentive. Sadiki's father translated the lean old muscular elder's words from Turkana to Swahili. He spoke words that blessed the boys' special friendship and recognized the close brother-like bond they had made with each other. Then the *mzee* strode up very close to Colin and took his hand, turning his palm up. As a special blessing and an intimate gesture of lasting friendship, he spat twice onto the little open palm. I was both moved by the tribute he paid Colin and mortified, thinking that Colin's first reaction might be to yank his hand back and yell out "yuck." Not anticipating the ritual, I hadn't prepared Colin for it. But the serious ceremonial aura surrounding the event profoundly conveyed its message to all of us and Colin seemed, without any coaching, to sense the special honor being bestowed on him. The little five year old stood quiet, tall, and respectful with his arm outstretched and his small hand open, held firm and tender by Sadiki's grandfather. Sadiki looked on quietly, seriously, and proudly.

The entire hillside community seemed to acknowledge the children's new language, seeing it as a special gift and a blessing from God; something sacred and a symbol of their new friendship. After just a few months together on this remote hillside, in a complex multilingual contact zone at the borders and limits of language and culture, these two five-year-old friends, one African and one American, from vastly different and strikingly unequal worlds, had formed a special bond and generated a unique means of speech that they called "Our Language."

Although I was deeply touched and moved by all of the loving attention to the children, the celebration of their friendship, and the affectionate embrace of my son, I was certain that this must all be a very big mistake. I knew this was impossible. I had been an elementary school teacher for six years. At that time I was a children's fiction writer and curriculum developer for a national educational research laboratory. I was also a part-time graduate student studying language acquisition and developmental psychology. I knew the current language development literature and the literature was very clear – two five year olds simply could not create a new language! In fact, according to Piaget,[8] egocentric five year olds could barely converse with each other. Piaget argued that they could not really modify or adjust their speech for interlocutors. He asserted that children of this age engaged in parallel monologues rather than genuine conversation. Although most parents could, based on their own direct observations, offer dozens of counterexamples demonstrating that young children are highly skilled and effective social communicators, Piagetian scholarly notions about children's egocentric speech were professionally widely accepted and unquestioned in 1975. I had studied these prominent child language theories. I had even identified myself as a Piagetian, which I considered a noble alternative to being a Skinnerian in those days. I was a member of the Piaget Society. Piaget and his distinguished colleagues, Hermina Sinclair De-Zwart and Barbel Inhelder, had been regular consultants at Research for Better Schools, Inc. (RBS), the nationally funded educational research laboratory in Philadelphia where I had been working as a writer since Colin's birth. I even kept a photograph of Piaget smoking his signature pipe and wearing his distinctive beret on my desk at RBS. How could these two five year olds possibly invent a shared language of their own? It simply wasn't developmentally possible. Piaget said so.

At that time, 40 years ago, in 1975, child language studies were still relatively new and largely influenced by Chomskian goals and research methods such as interview and elicitation (e.g., "repeat after me" or "say this"). Naturalistic and ethnographic studies of everyday child language behavior were not yet widely accepted or even seen as significant.[9] Cross-cultural knowledge about children's language development was only beginning to be explored[10] and little was known about children's actual language behaviors in language contact situations. Linguistic anthropologist Bambi Schieffelin was still in the field in Papua New Guinea conducting what was later to be published as her ground-breaking ethnographic study of Kaluli child language socialization.[11] Russian psychologist Lev Vygotsky's[12] more social and interactional understanding of the development of child language and thought was not yet translated or widely read by western scholars. The pivotal studies on the sociocentric language abilities of very young children by Marilyn Shatz and Rochelle Gelman[13] and Elinor Ochs Keenan,[14] which directly contradicted Piaget's assertions about egocentric speech, had not yet been written.

Given that none of these studies yet existed, and relying on Piaget's theories, I was fairly convinced that children were incapable of such a sophisticated linguistic innovation. I searched for other explanations. Oh no. Maybe it was the little mock language game I made up with Colin that was the source of all this confusion. When we first arrived in Kenya, we had spent a few weeks in Nairobi taking care of myriad bureaucratic tasks and details, getting permits, buying a vehicle, purchasing supplies, and preparing to go to our new field site. In cosmopolitan multilingual Nairobi, though English and Swahili were prominently spoken, we were surrounded by people speaking dozens of other local indigenous and international languages. Colin seemed a bit overwhelmed and confused by the new languages being spoken all around us. He seemed anxious to play with the two young German children we saw in the dining room at breakfast every morning at the old Ainsworth Hotel where we were staying. But the obvious language barrier and Colin's shyness limited anything more than just looking on at their play from a distance, then imitating what they were doing on his own, alone. Feeling a bit concerned and protective, I came up with a playful language game for the two of us. I reassured him that we could be like the many others all around us speaking languages other than English – like the Gujarati family who owned the restaurant where we frequently ate, the Swahili-, Luo-, and Kikuyu-speaking Africans we met daily, and the many European tourists dressed in fashionable safari outfits chatting in cacophonous choruses of Italian, French, and German that we overheard on the patio of the New Stanley Hotel, a convenient spot where we'd meet after doing various errands and Colin would guzzle strawberries and ice cream.

I suggested that we could speak "our own" special language too. I would utter a string of nonsense syllables with exaggerated intonation and dramatic prosody. Then Colin would do the same to answer me. We both had lots of fun with our highly animated nonsensical mock language game. Now I was horrified. I thought Colin must have been using the mock language when he played with Sadiki. Sadiki was probably deferring to and simply imitating him. Maybe they were both speaking a kind of playful gibberish in Piagetian parallel monologues?

Skeptical and not convinced that the children were really communicating, I decided to conduct a small experiment. I asked Sadiki to wait outside in the courtyard and instructed Colin that when Sadiki returned, Colin should give him specific verbal directions. I asked him to tell Sadiki to do things like "Turn around three times and sit in the blue chair." "Eat one cookie from the plate on the table." When Sadiki came back into the house, Colin repeated the directions. To my surprise, Sadiki followed each of the directions exactly! I did the same with Sadiki who also was able to have Colin follow his directions. They both did this all in a Swahili-sounding language that I could not understand. I was shocked but persuaded. I was finally convinced of what my neighbors already were certain of. The boys had actually created, and were speaking, a unique variety of speech that no one else could understand but the two of them. Piaget was wrong. I was captivated.

The word "serendipity" was coined by Horace Walpole, upon discovering a Persian fairy tale about three princes of "Serendip." In a letter to Horace Mann on January 28, 1754, Walpole described the princes as "always making discoveries, by accidents and sagacity, of things which they were not in quest of."[15] Many years later, drawing on this neologism, Robert K. Merton developed the notion of a "serendipity pattern" in social science research, referring to the common experience of having an unanticipated and anomalous observation that is both surprising and inconsistent with existing conceptions, ideas, facts, and theories. These unsought for discoveries provoke curiosity and subsequently further scientific inquiry. Merton also draws on Charles Sanders Peirce's related ideas about the strategic role of the "surprise fact" in his conception of "abduction" (as differentiated from induction and deduction), which leads to the logic of formulating newly invented explanatory hypotheses and new knowledge.[16]

At the time I witnessed Colin and Sadiki's language invention, I had not read Walpole, Merton, or Peirce, but I can vividly recall my complete shock and surprise at these events and my intense curiosity sparked by observing this unexplained linguistic marvel. The discovery of their surprising and unique language behaviors caused me to question all that I knew about child language. It provoked me to systematically pay even closer attention to what was happening in order to seek some orderly way to explain this startling, if not to my knowledge, impossible, phenomenon. Thus began my own serendipitous, unplanned and accidental study, prompting close and detailed observations of the children's daily interactions and ranging multilingual discursive practices in their numerous linguistic and cultural contexts.

I turned the tape recorder on and began to document and record the children. I recorded their interactions in a range of daily activities including dialogues at mealtime, indoor and outdoor play times, chatting in the back seat on car rides, and the like. I also had them record themselves when they were alone, hoping to compare their public and private interactions. In addition to my cassette recorder, Colin's father had brought some sensitive high-quality recording equipment for taping baboon vocalizations. Hugh helped me record the children's verbal interactions using his more sensitive sound equipment. Strongly influenced by Dell Hymes'[17] ethnography of communication approach, in addition to the recordings I kept detailed written records of my daily observations of their range of public and private, in and out group, and formal and informal social interactions with each other and with the variety of others they encountered on the hillside, at the local market, in shops in town, and later at their little preschool. I also documented our family's daily life experiences and routines in personal journals and letters. These written texts contained the ethnographic details of our everyday lives and the context and setting for the boys' unusual language practices. I was able to document the uses of their idiosyncratic private language over time from its early genesis through its ongoing use and expansion until the day we left to return to the United States, when their ephemeral pidgin ceased to be spoken.

The children's different language proficiencies and practices were dynamic and continuously changing over the course of the time we were there. I kept records of the range and frequency of uses of the different languages in their overlapping, collective, and steadily growing multilingual repertoires – English, Samburu, Up-Country Swahili as well as their own private language.

When we first arrived at Kekopey, Colin spoke English and had learned a few Swahili words. Joab, the project's long-time Abaluhya house servant and cook, who had run the Red House and graciously cared for the needs of its transient residents since the project began, took on the role of our family's *mwalimu* (teacher). With his gentle, kind, and patient encouragement, Colin was acquiring more and more Swahili. Colin developed increasing competence in Swahili and soon seemed able to speak with our African neighbors easily. Late one day at the end of our second month in the Red House, Joab, with an approving nod and smile, commented that Colin knew "*Swahili mingi*" (much Swahili). When I was observing the baboons nearby, Colin would sometimes stay alone with Joab, with whom he communicated only in Swahili. That is not to say that Colin's Swahili was fluent at that point. Though he could communicate his needs and generally feel confident about expressing himself, Colin's competence in Swahili was limited. He never needed a degree of proficiency beyond a certain level because, as is traditionally appropriate, his conversation with adults was limited, and because we were so isolated he did not often or regularly play with predominantly Swahili-speaking children. However, Colin's Swahili was good enough that when our car broke down on one of our first shopping trips to the nearby town of Nakuru, and we had to hitchhike home with our groceries, Colin assumed the role of translator and interpreter for me. The driver of the lorry (i.e., truck) who kindly picked us up understood Colin's Swahili much better than he did mine. Later Colin, trying to console me, said, "You know the words, Mom, but you don't have the voice for it." My voice did have a nasal resonance when speaking Swahili or, for that matter, English. Colin instead, when speaking Swahili, had picked up Sadiki's rich deep-toned chest resonance with utterances often delivered in command-like syllable stressed staccato tones. This stylistic "deep voice" made them both sound so confident and strong to me, especially for such young children.

Colin certainly didn't seem shy in this new environment. The African neighbors on the hill were very loving and would gently joke and tease with him in Swahili. He managed to respond and hold his own in these stylized humorous interactions. If they drank the milk of the *ngombe* (cow), what did he drink? Colin, even as a very young child, had a great sense of humor and a fast wit and could easily join the fun insisting that he drank the milk of the *nyani* (baboons). He not only demonstrated his competence in his limited but growing Swahili fluency but also in his appropriate performance as a participant in the gentle new teasing routine, a genre he was eagerly and confidently being socialized into.

Sadiki began the year fluent in Samburu, his home language and the language he spoke with his parents and siblings. He had some competence in Swahili but it was difficult to assess accurately his exact level of fluency. I suspected it was significantly more than he demonstrated. In keeping with cultural practice, Sadiki would not freely initiate talk or engage in lengthy conversations with adults. That would have been seen as disrespectful. (Occasionally his eyes would widen with surprise when Colin interacted with us by resisting or negotiating a request to clean his room, finish a meal, or get ready for bedtime; demanding our attention; asking for some indulgence, and the like. It was clear that from Sadiki's experience these were not only unfamiliar but inappropriate, almost outrageous, behaviors for children to engage in with adults.) Since there were rarely other Swahili-speaking children visiting the hillside, there were few opportunities to see him demonstrate his Swahili competence.

Sadiki was of course more proficient in Swahili than Colin. For example, in the early days of their friendship, in response to something Sadiki might say in Swahili, Colin would respond by repeating the phrase, "*Wewe sema nini?*" (What did you say?). Sadiki would often manage to find the words, gestures or actions that eventually would help Colin understand. But sometimes the frustration got to Colin and he would simply end the play session with an abrupt "*Kwa heri*" (Goodbye). I would witness these events with sympathy for Colin's frustration but concerned that he had a dismissive ring to his farewell and was not being considerate enough of Sadiki's feelings, and I would tell him so. Sadiki showed no outward signs of hurt or rejection if he felt them, but I thought he must have. He would simply repeat "*Kwa heri*" as he headed home. I'm sure they were both at times exasperated by their initial limited communicative proficiencies though I never saw Sadiki end a play session out of communicative frustration. But the frequency of these initial and obvious communication failures and frustrations seemed to dramatically decline by the end of the first few weeks.

Sadiki spent many long hours with our family. Although Colin's father and I spoke to Sadiki in Swahili, we spoke English to one another and to Colin. As the months passed Sadiki became quite competent in English though he rarely spoke it. Eventually his English seemed good enough that, with the enthusiastic approval of his parents, we arranged for him to attend a private English preschool with Colin. At the preschool it was expected that everyone speak English, and the British expatriate teacher was strict about the policy. The children both spoke and did their lessons in English at the school. Sadiki was able to navigate those English language spaces and tasks easily. He excelled there, demonstrating his competency not only with the English language but also with the range of appropriate interactional behaviors and classroom routines of this British school environment that was so new to and different for him.

Both children were eventually able to demonstrate appropriate bi- and trilingual code-switching abilities in each of their multiple overlapping linguistic communities. Many years later, this type of situation systematically occurring in Europe has been described under the rubric of superdiversity.[18] Both children spoke to Africans in Swahili. However, all interactions with one another were in their private language. They regularly demonstrated alternations and co-occurrences in their language use. For example, words quite familiar to them both in Swahili were regularly used when speaking to Africans. When speaking to each other in their private language, these same lexical items were replaced with their own newly invented words. In some cases, they actually invented numerous novel words for a single word they already knew and used regularly in Swahili. For example, while they knew, understood, and used the Swahili word *pesi pesi* (fast), they did not use it in their own language but actually created three new words that all meant *fast* – *diding*, *tena*, and *gningininga*. Not surprisingly, all of these newly invented words, or neologisms, sounded like the speeding car noises they made when they played together. They used these multiple sounds, which they had reshaped into onomatopoeia words, often and with visible playful pleasure. In addition to lexical code switching, they also shifted their language syntactically. In Up-Country Swahili, for example, the children would say *mpira yangu* (ball of mine – my ball) and in their language they would say *mimi mpira* (me ball – my ball).

The two continually played together mostly in isolation. Occasionally they played with Sadiki's sisters or other children who came to visit, but in general they spent most of their daylight hours playing with each other exclusively. One might speculate about whether their private language might have arisen if Colin had siblings or if Sadiki had brothers. Such factors would likely have dramatically altered the language equation.

Initially they shared only minimum competence in Swahili, the language they were expected to use when speaking across the language borders of the numerous compartmentalized self-contained speech communities on the hillside. As a result of not sharing a common language and out of necessity, Sadiki and Colin spontaneously generated a simplified means of speech that would serve their immediate communicative needs – what I identified as a Swahili pidgin, and they called "Our Language." Their private language sounded Swahili. Swahili was the dominant language and the language from which many of the loan words and most of the pronunciation patterns came. Aside from a few shared words, Samburu remained almost exclusively in Sadiki's repertoire and did not appear to be significantly represented lexically or syntactically in their language. Colin and Sadiki's language shared all of the basic linguistic features and characteristics of pidgin or contact languages all over the world. Like other pidgins, it is an admixture of both source languages (English and Swahili) and yet distinct from both. It reflects the simplification of forms typical of pidgins, including preverbal negation (e.g., *no run*), the absence of copula (i.e., the verb *to be*), articles (e.g., *the*, *a*) and inflection (e.g., grammatical word endings such as *-ed*, *-ing*). The lexicon is limited as is the function of the language. In Colin's words, "Well, you can't say *everything* in our language."

Though John Gumperz[19] had claimed that pidgin languages do not ordinarily serve as vehicles for personal friendships, it was clear that this was precisely what the two boys' pidgin was doing. Based on what little I knew and had read about contact languages, I assumed that their language was some variety of a simplified pidgin language. But no literature I knew of at that time suggested that it was possible that two children, without adult input, could create a pidgin by themselves. The literature generally claimed that children learned pidgins from adults.

As time passed, however, when other linguistic options were clearly available to each of them, namely English and Swahili, they maintained, continued to use, and continually expanded their private pidgin language with lexical expansion and sophisticated syntactic elaboration that was in fact more complex in some grammatical features than the local Up-Country Swahili. These complex linguistic innovations were suggestive of a nascent creolization or elaboration process that they accomplished in an extremely compressed time period. The process of creolization is characterized by an expansion of the pidgin, (re)introducing lexical and grammatical complexities that were reduced, simplified, and missing in the original pidgin, including a growing vocabulary, articles, markers, inflection, and copula, etc. Generally, the creolization process, the elaboration and complication of linguistic features, takes several generations and large populations to accomplish.

The persistence and elaboration of Sadiki and Colin's private language were particularly striking. Even though as time went by they were both demonstrating proficiency in and use of both English and Swahili, they did not stop using their language and instead were continually creating new lexical items and modifying their own novel syntactic constructions. I have recordings of the children inventing new lexical items four days before we left. It became clear that their language came to serve more than its initial pragmatic basic communicative function. Through their private language, they had constructed a separate speech community and a separate identity and they were determined to maintain both. None of the other language choices they had (i.e., English or Swahili) could accomplish those social functions.

As our arrival and the children's hillside encounter had marked the genesis of the boys' language, our leaving marked the end of their special private pidgin language. Once we returned to the United States, the boys' friendship continued primarily through letters written in English. Their spontaneous ephemeral language, which they had performed exclusively orally and in face-to-face interactions and was never written, ended its use the day we left the hillside speech situation.

I was able to take the data back with me to the States where I began to study with scholars in the field to discover what the children's language behavior was, what it meant and how they could have accomplished such complex language innovations. I realized later that I had only heard the children name their language in English. This was usually in response to my asking Colin something like "what are you speaking?" or "what was that?" I primarily directed my questions to Colin in the early days when I had just become aware of the existence of their language. The answer, "Our Language," was directed to me and therefore was always in English. In all the data I have collected, I have never found their own word for their language in their own language. Possibly they had one but I never heard it, didn't think to question them about it then, and today Sadiki doesn't remember anything other than the English, "Our Language." In earlier papers and publications, I referred to their language as "A Children's Pidgin (CP)" or "Colin and Sadiki's Pidgin." However, for the purpose of telling their full story in this book, Mikael Parkvall, a Swedish linguist and pidgin creole scholar with whom I had been corresponding, suggested to me, and I agreed, that the language should have its own name, in their own language. I set about constructing a translation of "Our Language" using the children's own lexical and grammatical rules.

In Kiswahili, the prefix *ki-* refers to the language itself. For example, the Swahili people speak Kiswahili, the Swahili language. (This is similar to the way *-ish* identifies the English, Danish, and Turkish languages.) The *ki-* prefix has also been used repeatedly to identify the many other language variations of Kiswahili, including Kisettla or Kisetta, the variety of language used by Africans and Europeans also known as Up-Country Swahili (also sometimes spelled KiSettla or KiSetta); Kivita, the war language which arose during World War II with the presence of Italian, French, and English troops in East Africa; Kishamba or plantation language; Kihindi, the Swahili variation used between Asians and Africans; and Kikar, the Swahili pidgin used as a lingua franca which served as a military jargon for the troops in the King's African Rifles (KAR) of British Colonial East Africa.[20] I chose the prefix *ki-* to name Colin and Sadiki's language. This was consistent with the practice of identifying and naming the wide range of other Swahili language varieties. The boys themselves often used this prefix, saying "Kisamburu" when referring to Sadiki's language.

But what morpheme, or meaningful unit of language, could follow *ki-* that might suggest "our" language? Colin and Sadiki's language didn't use the possessive "our." Further, they didn't distinguish between subject (e.g., I, we) and object (e.g., me, us) in their language. Their language used the objective case (e.g., me, us) to identify both the subject and object of the verb. "Our language" might therefore be translated as the "language (of) us." *Sisi* is the Swahili word for *we* or *us*, and also a word the children knew and sometimes used. *Sisi* also uses a repetitive reduplicated form that was a common feature in many of the children's newly invented words.

With Sadiki's amusement and approval in skype conversations, and following all of the linguistic rules of the boys' language, I named their language *Kisisi*. Though they didn't create the name, or ever actually utter the word, it sounds like something they might have said, and follows their own rule-governed language practices. I think Colin would have liked it too.

CHAPTER 2

HERODOTUS REVISITED: LANGUAGE ORIGINS, FORBIDDEN EXPERIMENTS, NEW LANGUAGES, AND PIDGINS

> It becomes evident that to ensure the creation of a speech which shall be a parent of a new lexical stock, all that is needed is that two or more young children should be placed by themselves in a condition where they will be entirely, or in a large degree, free from the presence and influence of their elders.
>
> Horatio Hale[1]

As a result of the children's prolonged hillside encounter, Sadiki and Colin, drawing on their own creative linguistic competencies and using the bits and pieces of multiple language resources circulating all around and between them, had somehow managed to negotiate their alterity through the invention of an original means of speech that enabled them to communicate quite facilely across their linguistic and cultural differences and their limited language proficiencies. The hillside residents were witness to the unanticipated birth of what they all recognized and spoke of as "a new language."

For centuries, speculations about the origins of human language (i.e., glottogenesis) and the birth of new languages have presented daunting questions for philosophers, language experts, historians, and scientists. Ironically, the primary reason for our being on this hillside in Kenya in the first place was to study nonhuman primate communication. Primate field studies at the time were in part driven by scientific fascination with questions about the

Kisisi (Our Language): The Story of Colin and Sadiki, First Edition. Perry Gilmore.
© 2016 Perry Gilmore. Published 2016 by John Wiley & Sons, Inc.

origin of language in the human species. The study of nonhuman primates in their natural habitat was considered to be a valuable potential source of information concerning possible models of early hominid behavior and communication. In the 1970s, long-term primate field studies were relatively new and made particularly well known by famous primatologists working in Africa, including Jane Goodall studying the chimps at Gombe in Tanzania and Dian Fossey studying gorillas in Uganda. Shirley Strum was one of the lead primatologists with whom we worked. She was a co-director, with Bob Harding, of the Gilgil Baboon Research Project. She joined us at the headquarters, in a tented annex adjacent to the Red House, for part of our stay. In addition to our own research, under her direction we learned the individual troop identities and maintained the project's daily records and ongoing data collection in her absence. In an article about the Pumphouse Gang in the *National Geographic* magazine, Strum stated, "By continuing our observations of nonhuman primate behavior, we can hope to gain a better understanding of ourselves: what we share with other primates, and what is uniquely ours."[2] One of those uniquely human behaviors was human language.

My own study focused on the acquisition and display of symbolic function, expressive repertoires, and social knowledge among the juvenile baboons. Specifically, I was looking for signs of symbolic function in the baboons' communicative repertoire, especially with regard to communication about and learning of their social rank. Piaget[3] had posited that nonhuman primates were incapable of symbolic function, and I had speculated that by conducting naturalistic observations of baboon behavior in the wild – as opposed to caged and lab studies that were so prevalent at the time – I might discover behaviors that would question these assumptions, especially about how juvenile baboons might learn, rather than inherit, their social rank.

Many of my Kenya research experiences – first with the baboons and then unexpectedly with the children – would eventually test my embrace of Piagetian theories.[4] This coming together was not about human and nonhuman primate cross-species encounters but about human-to-human encounters across the limitary boundaries of language.

The children's unique language situation was in many ways reminiscent of Herodotus' writings about the Egyptian Pharaoh Psamtik I and his infamous "forbidden experiment." What would happen if two young children who shared no language were isolated and deprived of language? Would they invent a language? What would that language be? What was the original human language?[5] The Pharaoh's experiment, conducted over 2000 years ago, sought to answer these philosophical questions about the origins of language by arranging for two infants to be raised in isolation without any exposure to language. A shepherd reportedly raised the infants in an isolated cottage. Threatened with death if he disobeyed, the shepherd followed strict instructions not to use or expose the infants to language of any kind – spoken, written, signed, or symbolic. When the children were about two years of age, they are said to have uttered the word *bekos*, interpreted as the word for "bread" in Phrygian. This lead Pharaoh Psamtik to conclude that Phrygian was the original mother language and that it predated Egyptian. Though 2000 years separated these events, I could not help but speculate about the odd but symbolic connection between first hearing the word *bekos* and first hearing the word *uweryumachini*.

Language deprivation or "forbidden" experiments have been conducted over the centuries for the purpose of discovering the fundamental character of humans and the origins of language.[6] Some of these studies, conducted by pharaohs, emperors, and kings, have also been identified as "royal investigations."[7] In addition to the Herodotus report of Psamtik I in the seventh century BC, other royal experiments were conducted by Frederick II of Sicily (1192–1250), James IV of Scotland (1473–1513), and India's Akbar the Great (1542–1605). They were all said to have designed experiments in which children were isolated from birth and deprived of exposure to any language in order to discover answers to these language origin questions. While the reports of these experiments are questionable in terms of their veracity, they are generally consistent with regard to their intent and their design. They are all considered "forbidden" because of the extreme and tragic nature of deprivation they demanded. In several cases it was reported that the children did not survive. Consider that if one denies language to the innocent children who are the subjects of study in these experiments, they are also in most cases being deprived of the human love and social interaction that are inextricably embedded in and inseparable from the language experience and the human condition.

Feral children have also long been of special fascination to the scientific community because it was thought they too might provide insight into questions of language origins, language acquisition, and critical periods for language development.[8] Since rescued feral children had already been isolated from human interaction and language by whatever cruel circumstances they had endured before they were found, the researchers themselves were not specifically designing a deprivation experiment. While there are many such unfortunate cases described in the literature,[9] two particularly poignant ones are widely known and carefully documented.

The wild boy of Aveyron was discovered in the woods near Saint Sernin, a village in southern France, in 1798. The naked boy, assumed to be about 11 or 12 years old, had likely been abandoned as a very young child and seemed to have survived on his own in the woods for years. The boy was eventually taken into the care of Jean Marc Gaspard Itard, a physician and researcher, who gave him the name "Victor." Itard documented his systematic, but in his own view unsuccessful, attempts to teach the boy language.[10]

Almost 200 years later, Francios Truffaut depicted Victor's poignant case in his 1970 film *The Wild Child*. The same year Truffaut's film was released, "Genie," often called "the modern day wild child," was rescued from an abusive, neglectful, and socially isolating situation where she too had had minimal exposure to human language.[11] Genie, like Victor, was the subject of close and lengthy study as attempts were made to teach her language. Tragically, both children seemed to suffer not only in their initial isolated circumstances but also at the hands of possibly well-meaning but ethically misguided researchers who had these children work and train intensely but never were fully pleased with the limited language advances the children actually made. Sadly, the researchers, working two centuries apart, in each case made no personal commitment to the long-term well-being of either "wild child" beyond their funded language training experiments.[12]

In 1977, Derek Bickerton, a linguist who specializes in pidgin and creole studies, designed a language experiment quite similar to the Herodotus experiment and the other forbidden experiments mentioned above. His variation of the experiment was to bring together families who spoke a variety of different languages in order to create a language contact zone that might produce a pidgin/creole genesis. In his book, *Bastard Tongues*, he describes his "forbidden experiment" in great detail.[13] He and his colleague, Talmy Givón, proposed to recruit six young families, each family being speakers of different unrelated languages but with no exposure to any "metropolitan" languages. The families were ideally to have children who were two years old and developmentally ready or just beginning to acquire language. The families would live together on Ngemelis, a small western Pacific atoll in the Palau islands, for one year where they would go about the business of living and raising their small children under very close observation. The linguists were counting on the inevitability that as "the parents grew coconuts, the children would grow a language."[14] Bickerton planned to prepare a "starter vocabulary" of about 200 words for the participants, hoping to "step up the pace of linguistic evolution" and start a new creole. Their goals were to "determine whether either children or adults were capable of inventing grammatical structures, ways of forming sentences that were not modeled on anything they'd ever heard."[15]

Bickerton proposed that he, his colleagues, and their graduate students would be there to record and document the linguistic birth process of a pidgin/creole language and to discover the specific roles adults and children played in its genesis. Their proposal to the National Science Foundation was most controversial and not surprisingly denied because of the many ethical concerns it raised about the exploitation, safety, and psychological well-being of their "subjects." One of the proposal reviewers commented, "The project is unethical, racist, and exploitative, particularly given the fact that the subjects are to be from areas with little or no contact with the Western world ... the Pacific is not a cultural zoo."[16] Bickerton was angered by and highly critical of their final decision not to fund the experiment. He has continued to speculate about the possibility of creating this ultimate experiment in ways that might get around the human subjects restrictions. Over the years he has suggested a variety of other possible design models, including recruiting white European families,[17] raising orphans in South America, and setting up special urban day care centers in the United States for children of recent immigrants.[18] All of the designs would require that the child participants would have very limited and highly restricted language input from adults and other children. None of these experiments has ever been implemented. In the end, most researchers would agree that these projects as described are deeply problematic and highly unethical. These experiments, after all, have been called "forbidden" for good reason.

At a recent anthropology meeting, I was introduced to Christina Higgins, a sociolinguist at the University of Hawaii, who had worked in Tanzania and Kenya studying how multilingual individuals use English along with local languages to produce their own unique local and global identities.[19] She had been told about the boys' language invention and asked me about it. As I started to briefly describe Sadiki and Colin's language creation to her, she interrupted, chiming in, "Oh, Bickerton's dream experiment!" making the quick comparison.

Indeed, Sadiki and Colin's language genesis experience could be viewed as a much happier version of Bickerton's forbidden experiment. Their experience could be seen as a kind of "natural" experiment where in fact many of the variable factors detailed in Bickerton's proposal were part of their natural speech situation. But in the boys' experience the conditions were controlled by happenstance and serendipity rather than by design. Their experience was also completely voluntary, motivated and sustained by play and friendship rather than contract or mandate. But the living conditions Sadiki and Colin experienced on the remote multilingual hillside did share many of the extreme social and linguistic factors that were seen as essential in the "forbidden" design of Bickerton's proposal. The two boys were living in a very isolated and remote multilingual context in the Kenya bush, thrust together by chance in a polylingual linguistic contact zone and sharing no common language. Though they were surrounded, loved, and supported by family and community, the boys played together alone, without adults or other children present, for very long hours every day. Their highly exclusive and continuous play created a fertile space for their pidgin genesis. However, their speech situation could not have been orchestrated or planned nor could it have been unembedded from the complex asymmetrical hegemonic postcolonial social and cultural dynamic in which it was firmly and deeply planted and in response to which their resistant language practices thrived. The unequal social conditions no doubt acted as a strong motivating catalyst for their sustained language creations.

Two additional studies are relevant to a discussion of language origins. Both are, like Colin and Sadiki's experience, naturally occurring. These are both cases of new languages that have provided provocative insights into questions about language origins and especially the role of children as language innovators. The first case, a widely recognized study of children's language innovation, is the invented sign language of deaf Nicaraguan school children created through contact at the government boarding schools for the education of deaf children that opened in the late 1970s and early 1980s after the Sandinista revolution. Their unique peer-generated sign language has been studied closely by linguists who have analyzed its emergence, development, and changes over time.[20] The Nicaraguan children's sign language invention has been described as peer driven and seen as part of the youth's resistance to the imposition of the formal school's deaf sign language curriculum. The first stage, Lenguaje de Signos Nicaragüense (LSN), of Nicaraguan Sign Language has been identified as "pidgin-like" and compared to an "expanded pidgin."[21] Later, when new and younger speakers entered the school population, the sign language developed more creole-like complexity and syntactic elaborations. The second creole-like stage has been called Idioma de Señas de Nicaragua (ISN).

Initially, the staff at the school saw these creative gestural behaviors through a deficit lens, assuming it was evidence of their failed attempts to learn Spanish sign language. It was not until 1986, when linguist Judy Kegl, a PhD from the Massachusetts Institute of Technology, was brought in to help them understand the children, that the language was actually identified as a distinct, invented, and systematic new peer sign language. Noted psychologist Steven Pinker states, "The Nicaraguan case is absolutely unique in history. We've been able to see how it is that children – not adults – generate language, and we have been able to record it happening in great scientific detail. And it's the only time that we've actually seen a language being created out of thin air."[22] While Pinker's claims and enthusiasm are completely appreciated, I suggest that the children's sign language was not actually created "out of thin air." The children had come from homes where, in the absence of any other learned code or formal sign language, most of their families had, out of both necessity and intimacy, developed a range of simple and complex gestures to form at least rudimentary and original "home" sign languages in order to routinely communicate.[23] This rich range of original communicative gestural systems was most likely brought together in what must have been a unique multisigning system contact zone at the boarding schools where the children constructed their new speech communities. These home sign languages offered real and situated gestural forms deployed as part of the communicative resources for the pidgin-like sign system that the children ultimately created.

Another more recent study of naturally occuring language invention was conducted by linguist Carmel O'Shannessy,[24] who documented a new language variety she discovered that had been created by children living in a remote village in northern Australia. Her study of the language, Light Warlpiri, is an examination of a new language in what she identifies as the early period of its existence. She speculates that the language is probably about 35 years old and now spoken exclusively by the younger generation in the community. The role of children as language innovators and creators of Light Warlpiri has been a significant focus in her research.

These two studies highlight the contribution of youth to language creation and the value of documenting such rarely occurring linguistic phenomena. The Nicaraguan and Light Warlpiri studies had not been conducted or published at the time Sadiki and Colin invented Kisisi. However, it is interesting to compare Kisisi with these two cases now. Consider, for example, that both the Nicaraguan sign language and Light Warlpiri have been continuously used and developing for decades whereas Kisisi was short-lived, only developed and used while the children were in close face-to-face proximity. Kisisi was a language variety created and used exclusively by only two children in isolation as opposed to the larger and generational peer populations described in the Australian and Nicaraguan cases. In the Light Warlpiri study, O'Shannessy, estimating that the new language is about 35 years old, claims that it is a young language and in its early stages of development. Sadiki and Colin's language became noticeable and identified by the larger community as a unique "language" within just a few months of its genesis and continued to considerably expand and develop lexically and syntactically in its very brief lifetime. The speed of Kisisi's initial genesis and complex syntactic creole-like development is quite striking by comparison.

Kisisi, unlike the Light Warlpiri and Nicaraguan cases, provides not only linguistic but also detailed sociolinguistic and ethnographic data for a closer, nuanced, and processual examination of language genesis from its earliest development *in situ* and *in vivo*. I began recording the children and documenting the range of functions, uses, and meanings of Kisisi as soon as I realized the boys were speaking a unique variety. Therefore, minus the first 8–10 weeks when I assumed that they were interacting in Up-Country Swahili, the study of Kisisi documents the language as it was actually emerging. The Kisisi study produced an archive of the dynamic evolution of a pidgin-in-the-making. As a parent ethnographer in this accidental study, I was intimately positioned in a participant observer role, able to capture in detail the dynamic, complex, and nuanced political, cultural, and social aspects of this tiny speech community of two as well as documenting the language's continuously changing structural features.

In both the Australian and Nicaraguan examples, the language innovations were accomplished by large peer groups, but there are also numerous cases in the literature of only two or three children who, like Sadiki and Colin, created private idiosyncratic languages. The reports of these cases are mostly anecdotal, often identifying siblings living in remote areas. Contrasted with Piaget's widely held and popular view of children as egocentric language users, as early as 1886 Horatio Hale[25] had actually observed quite the opposite, noting the language-creating tendencies of very young children. He theorized that if two or three children were together and entirely, or to a large degree, free from adult influence, they would be likely to create a new language. He reported five cases that he had come across where young children in fact did so. Unfortunately, only scant examples of invented lexical items are offered in these early reports. Otto Jespersen, a Danish linguist, keenly interested in these cases as they related to understandings about the nature and origins of language, noted that in all Hale's reported cases, "the children seem to have talked together fluently when by themselves in their own gibberish."[26]

In 1903 Jespersen had the opportunity to directly witness the use of a private language by twin boys in Denmark. He was lecturing at the University of Copenhagen when he was told about twin boys living not too far away who had developed a private language. He was able to spend time with and directly observe the five and a half-year-old twin boys. Their language, and their state of neglect, were discovered when they were four and they were subsequently sent to a children's home. Jespersen made several visits to the home, spending time with them and learning some of their language. He reports that the boys were shy with other children. They seemed to understand "many everyday sentences spoken to them … but they could not speak Danish and said very little in the presence of anybody else." Jespersen observed, however, that when the twins were alone, they conversed freely in their own "gibberish" which he referred to as an "idiom" rather than a "complete or fully developed language."[27] Both Hale and Jespersen noted that the common conditions for these cases included parents who "spoilt" or "neglected" their children. In all of these cases of idioglossia, the children were very young when they developed their shared language – two to three years old – and attempting to converse in what was their first language and not proficient in any other language(s).

A much more recent and widely publicized study of twin idioglossia was the case of the Kennedy twins (Poto and Cabengo) identified in San Diego in 1977.[28] They had been assumed to be of limited intelligence and subsequently neglected and also not sent to school. A family caseworker, once made aware of their situation, sent them to the Children's Hospital of San Diego for speech therapy. There the speech therapists soon discovered that the twins were in fact of normal intelligence and their speech was not an example of the lack of language or low intelligence. Instead, they found that the twins actually had invented and were speaking a complex private language. Linguistic analysis showed that their language combined English, their parents' language, and German, the language of their grandmother who primarily cared for them. The language was described as containing many neologisms and unique grammatical features. Their father ultimately forbade the children from speaking their private language at the age of eight. They continued to develop their English language skills and were eventually mainstreamed and placed in separate classes in school.

In an interview in *Forbes* magazine, Noam Chomsky mentions a case discovered by several cognitive psychologists at the University of Pennsylvania. He recalled that there were three or four deaf children, possibly cousins, of speaking parents who all played together regularly. The parents, it seems, were all committed to the once popular use of oral language approaches which emphasized lip reading and frowned upon the use of any sign language or gesturing. The children, never having been exposed to any signing or even improvised gestures, apparently at the age of about three or four developed a home sign language. Chomsky states, "When it was investigated, it was found that it had the properties of normal language for children of their age. Of course, as soon as this was found they were immediately taught sign language, and the experiment was over."[29]

There are major distinguishing factors in Colin and Sadiki's private language creation and these examples of sibling, cousin, and twin idioglossia. Consider that Sadiki and Colin were a few years older than the children in these cases and both of them were already fully competent in their first languages (and in Sadiki's case, some degree of Swahili in addition to his Samburu fluency) before meeting and generating their pidgin. Further, after they had invented their private pidgin they were each able to demonstrate translanguaging abilities, continually and appropriately code switching bi- and trilingually. In most of the documented cases of idioglossia, the children were unable to code switch or speak other languages.[30]

Few examples of idioglossia have been closely observed *in situ*, recorded, or actually documented as they occurred. When they have been identified, they have usually been seen as pathological oddities, understood as disabilities that needed to be remediated. Mostly parents or caretakers were also harshly judged as neglectful in these reports. In striking contrast, Colin and Sadiki's language was viewed by their community as something sacred, cherished, and celebrated as a gift from God. The language itself was seen as more complicated and its speakers more competent, leaving the nonspeakers deficient and unable to understand. Kisisi was seen as a symbol of the boys' special love for each other, and as a result closely bonded their two families. These differences reveal much about the language ideologies that surrounded their speech situation. I recall joking about being relieved that the children invented their private language in Up-Country Kenya and not in our neighborhood back in the United States, where the discovery of their language would have no doubt been quickly diagnosed by the school as an indication of a learning disability followed immediately by a mandatory remediation plan and a strong concern about our parenting ablities. Sacred in one context, pathological in another. Seen as status enhancing and a sign of advanced linguistic complexity and love on the hillside; potentially seen as a stigmatized deficiency, a pathological problem, and a qualification for disability tracking in most mainstream US educational contexts.

There have, no doubt, been many undocumented instances of new speech varieties created in similar circumstances. However, linguists in the past had too often ignored children's language as imperfect, not fully developed, and therefore irrelevant to the study of linguistics. For example, William Samarin, a noted pidgin and creole scholar, after reading a 1979 paper of mine describing the children's pidgin,[31] kindly and enthusiastically wrote to me encouraging my research and sharing that in 1956 his three-year-old daughter had "developed, in interacting with her older African playmate, a pidgin based on Sango, English, French, and Gbeya."[32] Sadly he did not document their language. He wrote, "Unfortunately, that was before the days of convenient tape recorders!" I could not help but wonder how the distinguished author of *Field Linguistics: A Guide to Linguistic Field Work*,[33] *A Grammar of Sango*,[34] and an expert in salient and substantive pidginization processes[35] did not document his own daughter's language at the same time he was meticulously documenting the creole grammar of Sango. Samarin's experience seems to reflect not his own disinterest in the children's creativity, but the low status that child language studies held in linguistics at the time. The focus was on adult language and grammar. At that time, there was not as keen a linguistic interest in the processes of the language's development or in the individuals who were creating and using the language, especially if those individuals were children.

An unexpected and highly relevant example of a spontaneous speech variety was offered to me more recently by Bob Harding, the first primatologist to study the baboons on Kekopey. Bob originally established contact with the Cole family and initiated the baboon research in 1970. Bob, his wife Diana, and their two daughters, three-year-old Alexandra and 11-month-old Eliza, lived on the hillside for 14 months. Their little daughter, Eliza, was almost a year old when they arrived and just a little over two when they left. She first began to speak while they were living on the hillside. There were different resident workers on the hill during the time they lived there. Eliza spent many hours in the care of their Kipsigis *ayah* (nursemaid), whose husband was in charge of fence-building on the ranch. He also had a second wife who had a young toddler, David. The two children often played together under the watchful eye of the *ayah*. Bob wrote, "As far as we could tell, what she spoke with David was a combination of English, Kipsigis and Swahili ... We too heard that by the time we left, David and Eliza were speaking a language of their own that was unintelligible to anyone else. But since neither of us was linguistically trained and spoke only some upcountry Swahili and no Kipsigis, we did not pursue the matter at all. What a wasted research opportunity!"[36] According to Bob, their older daughter did not understand and never used the shared "language" that Eliza and David spoke to each other. The very similar experiences of the Harding family suggest that this particular hillside multilingual setting was quite conducive to creative language innovation, code mixing, and translanguaging where the children used all the language resources available to them in their diverse repertoires as a unified and integrated system with which to communicate. It confirms that the conditions on this hillside could foster new language development for children who were speakers of different languages living there. It is another example of the ways in which young children in multilingual contact situations regularly accommodate, play with, improvise, and create language in order to communicate.

The case of Colin and Sadiki's language invention provides a concrete and closely documented example of a language-in-the-making. Their experience offers evidence of the often unrecognized and underestimated language virtuosity of young children. Their story provides a brief glimpse at the creation of a language as it was happening "here and now"[37] and within the context of their everyday lived social and cultural experiences.

I identified Sadiki and Colin's private language as a spontaneous Swahili pidgin language, noting that Kisisi is a case of young children *inventing* a new pidgin language as opposed to children *learning* an existing pidgin language from adults.[38] I have repeatedly referred to pidgin and creole languages in the discussions above. But what exactly is a pidgin language and how does it differ from a creole? Although scholars recognize the problems in defining even the most basic concepts of language,[39] defining pidgin and creole languages can be all the more challenging.[40] Parkvall[41] asserts that there is no generally accepted definition of pidgin languages and offers instead common core properties. With these caveats expressed, I offer below a brief description of pidgins and creoles for the benefit for the reader.

Most commonly, a pidgin language is recognized as a reduced and simplified language that arises in extended contact situations where individuals have no common language and develop a means of restricted communication that will serve their limited needs. Extended contact might arise in circumstances of "discovery, exploration, trade, conquest, slavery, migration, colonialism, nationalism"[42] to name a few. No one's first language, pidgins are characterized by having temporarily pared down many of the inessential features of standard[43] or input languages.[44] Some of the features often absent in pidgins include articles, markers, inflection, and copula. Lexical stock is limited and usually reflects the restricted communicative needs of the speakers. The "simplification" process is similar to the linguistic accommodation that occurs in a number of other linguistic phenomena such as early childhood language,[45] motherese,[46] baby talk, lover talk, talk to foreigners and the deaf,[47] and second language acquisition.[48] These situations often produce a linguistic shift to what has been called a "simple register" sharing many of the features described above for pidgins.[49]

Where a pidgin functions to serve limited contact needs, a creole serves as a primary language in a speech community. As the creolization process progresses, the original pidgin will undergo change in response to the growing needs of its speakers to communicate about a full range of human experience with a richer lexicon and more grammatical complexity.[50] Hymes noted that it is the nature of a pidgin to either develop or to disappear.[51]

My late husband, linguistic anthropologist David Smith, observed "strikingly parallel processes"[52] in a child's development of communicative competence, moving from a pidginized to a creolized speech. I had met David and read several of his articles the year before I went to Kenya. His research had made a strong impression on me. I know that having read his papers on pidgin and creole processes heightened my awareness of the significance of the children's language practices and motivated my interest in documenting their simplification and elaboration patterns. I planned to, and later did, take these data back to work with noted anthropologists, sociolinguistics, and pidgin/creole scholars at the University of Pennsylvania, including David Smith, Dell Hymes, Bill Labov, Erving Goffman, Gillian Sankoff, and Bambi Scheiffelin, to seek their expertise and tutelage in analyzing what the children had been doing with language.

In more recent years, scholars have continued to do work to strengthen the connections between language acquisition and creolization.[53] In the pidgin–creole continuum, one would therefore find the constant interplay of the two processes of reduction and simplification as well as expansion and complication – or pidginization and creolization.[54] Hymes emphasized the significance of the processes of simplification and elaboration in these dynamic language phenomena. He notes that the "awkward but accurate"[55] title of his edited volume, *Pidginization and Creolization of Langauges*, spoke to that focus. Instead of using the nouns pidgin and creole, the volume title featured the words pidginization and creolization, focusing on the verb-like aspects of such dynamic processes as language origins, development, maintenance, contact, hybridization, convergence, acculturation, and evolution. In a similar spirit and also emphasizing process, David Smith chose to identify pidgin and creole languages as "acculturating languages"[56] to escape these central problems of definition and variation and to capture the ever-changing nature of language in use, especially in the range of contact situations and multilingual hybrid speech communities where these "means of speech" most frequently arise.

Jourdan writes, "Just as cultures develop over time, so do the pidgin languages that become their linguistic medium. Languages cannot exist without the cultures that sustain them, and they cannot develop before the cultures that sustain them develop; the two go hand in hand, in a form of constant feedback, through which social groups become encultured and enlanguaged."[57]

Hymes has argued that the study of pidgin and creole contact languages can make significant contributions to linguistic and social theory and to a deeper understanding of central questions about the very nature of human language, social interaction, and meaning making.[58] Examination of the emergence, development, and everyday uses of contact languages and their linguistic varieties provides insight into the construction of language identities and ideologies, the uses of language practices as performances of social agency, and the processes of negotiating linguistic hybridity in stance saturated global multilingual zones of contact and interaction.

Pidgin and creole languages frequently originated in colonial settings and within stark hegemonic social arrangements (e.g., plantation systems, slavery, discovery, conquest, migration), their speakers representing the least powerful members of society.[59] While relationships between colonial contexts and language varieties have long been of interest to many pidgin and creole scholars, there is growing attention to the interdisciplinary study of colonial and postcolonial linguistics.[60] The field explores both "how language is affected by colonial and postcolonial conditions and how colonial and postcolonial constellations of facts are reflected, shaped and negotiated by language."[61] The genesis of hybrid language varieties in language contact zones, including so-called pidgin and creole languages, is a relevant topic of inquiry. Pratt has identified "contact zones" as "social spaces where cultures meet, clash, and grapple with each other, often in contexts of highly asymmetrical relations of power, such as colonialism, slavery, or their aftermaths as they are lived out in many parts of the world today."[62]

Dell Hymes drew broad scholarly attention to the significant scientific contribution the study of pidgin and creole languages can make. He writes, "These languages demonstrate dramatically the interdependence of language and society. Their study opens up new possibilities for integration of linguistic and social research."[63] Hymes called for studies of specific cases of pidgins and creoles to generate a more comparative model of their formation not only across linguistic connections but also across common social factors.

The study of Colin and Sadiki's language responds to his call. This accidental study generated concrete empirical data documenting the discursive processes they employed to generate, shape, negotiate, and sustain membership in their exclusive two-member speech community. The creation of this original pidgin language marked the simultaneous creation of a new space in their existing multilingual, compartmentalized, and highly stratified speech community.[64] Membership in the boys' new speech community in turn provided a place within which they could represent and actualize their shared identities, ideologies and agency, a site for resistance, solidarity, and transformation. This representative place for their friendship allowed them to mediate and transcend the racialized hegemonic linguistic and cultural borders that enveloped them in postcolonial Kenya. Enacted in a setting with historically distinct and oppressive colonizing histories, their case presents a provocative extreme along a continuum of possibilities in examining language choices and behaviors in social practice. The example also provides a lens for understanding how young members of language communities use and think about language – how they exercise language choice, change, and possibility.

The role of young children as language innovators, pidgin creators and creolizers, and *de facto* language policy makers has been largely understudied, undocumented, and even ignored. In pidgin and creole studies, it is largely assumed that the "adults are the *innovators* whereas the children are the *regulators*."[65] Colin and Sadiki's creative language inventiveness demonstrates that children can be exceptional language innovators. This case of language invention provides documentation of children's language creativity, gives insight into the agentive roles of children as language innovators in multilingual contact situations, and sheds new light on questions of language genesis, change, shift, and maintenance. This case documents the birth, expansion, and eventual loss and death of an ephemeral Swahili pidgin language.

Initially, when the two children met, they shared only minimum competence in Swahili, the local language they were expected to converse in. As a result and out of necessity, they generated a pidgin that served their immediate communicative needs. However, as time passed, and they had become fluent in the other languages available to them, namely English and Swahili, instead of abandoning their pidgin, they continued to use, expand, and creolize their private language. What is quite remarkable is that this unique contact language was *not* generated by a large adult community gradually over several generations, as is most common for pidgin and creole languages. Instead, and in striking contrast to most of the existing literature on new languages, the spontaneous genesis was accomplished by two young five year olds and, astonishingly, in only a few months' time. The young language inventors, who played together daily, continually expanded their initial pidgin, continuously inventing new lexical items and grammaticalizing their language in ways that are typical of the language changes in large populations over multiple decades and across generations. Their language provides a detailed look at the boys' sociolinguistic communicative competencies as they navigated the complex multilingual hegemonic borderlands in the challenging sociopolitical context of Kenya's early years of independence. The discussion of the boys' language explores the range of linguistic mechanisms of invention the children drew on to create their unique private language. The description of their experiences also demonstrates how the children's ongoing discursive language invention enabled them to resist and challenge the persisting colonial ideologies that oppressed and surrounded them; transcend highly stratified unequal social, economic, and racial power arrangements; and transform the social order and cultural practices that potentially constrained their relationships.

A final provocative example that should be highlighted in relation to Kisisi is the growing language phenomenon of Sheng, a new spontaneous and fast-growing variety of Kiswahili that primarily mixes English and Swahili with a sprinkling of words from other local languages. Sheng echoes many of the linguistic features and social functions of Kisisi, which also drew primarily from the source languages of Swahili and English and also evolved in response to the colonial multilingual context in Kenya. Since the recent spread and popularity of Sheng in Kenya, people who have heard or read about Colin and Sadiki's language have even suggested to me that it seemed as though the two boys were "Shenging."

I first learned about Sheng in the mid-1980s when Andrew Hill, a friend and at the time a research paleontologist at the National Museums of Kenya in Nairobi, seeing the immediate connection between the boys' language and Sheng, sent me a March 14, 1984 copy of *The Daily Nation* which featured an article by Catherine Gicheru and Roy Gachuhu headlined "SHENG: New Urban Language Baffles Parents." The authors explain Sheng in the following way, "To coin the word they have taken the letters 'S' and 'H' from Swahili and added the 'eng' of the word English." They go on to describe the multilingual situation where multiethnic youth in the city, so many of whom cannot speak either English or Swahili fluently, reach "a kind of compromise and come up with Sheng ... To ensure that they can at least communicate with their peers, most of the children cling to Sheng ..."[66] The authors express a very positive view of the new language offering: "But the beauty of Sheng is really its capacity to translate what people hear, see and feel into a vivid life experience ... Sheng is beauty. Sheng is fun. And Sheng is easy to learn."[67] This newspaper article appeared almost 10 years after the boys had created their language. In their experiences on Kekopey and their rural life in Up-Country Kenya, Sadiki and Colin had no exposure to Sheng, which was at that time not well known, not widespread, and largely restricted to poor residential areas outside Nairobi.

Sheng was spoken originally by urban youth in Eastlands, a poor multiethnic and multilingual residential area outside the city of Nairobi. Identified as early as the 1950s, this urban youth language has in more recent decades evolved and spread more widely to other Kenyan towns and diverse populations and has become broadly used by music artists and popular media.[68] Sheng, like Kisisi, is not a written language and is not taught in schools but instead is primarily generated and shared by peers. Competing views have variously described Sheng as a pidgin, a creole, code switching, a Swahili dialect, slang, a street language, a mixed language, an antilanguage,[69] and a hybrid language.[70] Sheng is described by Orcutt-Gachiri[71] as having a strong anti-tribalist stance, incorporating words from the range of Kenya's mother tongues in a celebratory embrace of Kenya's linguistic and cultural diversity. Mazuri argues that Sheng defies these classifications "because although it exhibits features that characterize all these categories, none can be said to exhaustively capture its various peculiarities."[72]

Bosire identifies the hybrid languages of Africa as "contact outcomes that have evolved at a time when African communities are coming to terms with the colonial and postcolonial situation that included rapid urbanization and bringing together of different ethnic communities and cultures with a concomitant exposure to different ways of being ... Sheng is a culmination of a hybridization process, which Bakthin has described as 'a mixture between two different linguistic consciousnesses, separated from one another by an epoch, by a social differentiation, or by some other factor'."[73] In this case, Sheng serves not only as a lingua franca of the metropolis but also to facilitate egalitarianism.[74] This anti-language rejects English, the language of colonialism, Kiswahili, the language of coastal Islam and the slave trade, and the connotations of rusticity and inferiority of Up-Country Swahili and Kishamba.

David Samper describes Sheng as a hybrid language that "gives young people the wherewithal to question and challenge the ideologies and identities that attempt to define them."[75] He defines hybridity as a lived and performed practice where "Hybrid forms and identities reflect an intentional re-voicing of cultural elements and conscious re-fashioning and re-imaging of the self. Hybridity does not describe changes in a global society; it describes a process of creatively manipulating culture and identity. Hybrid forms and identities are thus a performed 'cultural cut'n mix'."[76] He notes that hybrid expressions, like Sheng, are products of linguistic, cultural, and racial boundary transgressions. Drawing on the work of Bakhtin[77] and Bhabba,[78] Samper identifies Sheng's hybridity as being "characterized as double voiced, dialogic and heteroglossic ... The concept is imbued with liminality; hybrid forms inhabit a cultural middle/border/contact zone, a third space, that is 'in-between' and yet 'beyond' its constituent parts. Being in-between is ambiguous, marginal space which nonetheless grants the hybrid expression mocking, ironic, and ultimately subversive power ... [enabling the] destabilization or subversion of hierarchical power."[79] Sheng participates in the formation of a youth culture identity with its own lifestyle and ideology. Samper concludes that, "Young people use Sheng to define themselves, to symbolize their distinctiveness, to express their worldview and to reflect on their own cohesiveness."[80]

In these ways, Sheng and Kisisi are very much alike. They are both secret and exclusive. They both contest and function in direct opposition to the dominant colonial and postcolonial social system. Like other anti-languages,[81] they function to reject the languages of the privileged and exclude their speakers. Sheng and Kisisi create a social reality[82] for their speakers. The languages are both symbols of identity, group membership, and solidarity as well as a functional code for expressing feelings, attitudes, and loyalties.

Linguistically, there are some interesting similarities and captivating contrasts. Sheng's inventiveness is focused largely in the development of an extensive creative vocabulary drawing on devices such as compounding, borrowing, truncation, semantic shifting, affixation, and metathesis. Kisisi also heavily employs compounding, borrowing, and truncation but Kisisi differs in its uses of a great deal of soundplay, onomatopoeia, and reduplication in creating neologisms. In Sheng, there is very little creativity in the grammar, which has no articles, omits relative pronouns, and overuses the simple present tense using the Kiswahili present tense marker *na-* and omitting the past marker *li-* and future marker *ta-*. The overuse of the present tense has been described as contributing to the vivid, picturesque, and cinematographic effect of Sheng.

In striking contrast, Kisisi has elaborated its grammatical structure, developing original articles and pronouns and tense and aspect markers to distinguish both when events occur on the axis of time and the ability to describe the ontology of events as accomplished or unaccomplished, durative or nondurative, etc. It is most interesting that the two five-year-old Kisisi speakers are more inventive in the complex area of syntax than the large adolescent youth population of Sheng speakers. The complexity of Kisisi's grammatical innovations seems most sophisticated by comparison to the oversimplified grammar of Sheng. This dramatically highlights the creative linguistic competencies of very young children and their often overlooked potential as language innovators and pidgin creolizers.

Each of these many examples from the literature – including forbidden experiments, idioglossia, pidgins and creoles, hybrid languages, mixed languages, and new languages – explores profound questions about the origin of language. The case of Kisisi, the original language that Colin and Sadiki invented, adds to this literature and sheds light on questions about the contribution of young children to language invention and development.

CHAPTER 3

LORCA'S MIRACLE: PLAY, PERFORMANCE, VERBAL ART, AND CREATIVITY

Tell me what you play and I'll tell you who you are.

Roger Callois[1]

Word and idea are not born of scientific or logical thinking but of creative language ...

Johan Huizinga[2]

The discussion thus far has addressed areas in the literature quite familiar to academic inquiry concerning language origins and acquisition – primate communication, royal investigations, forbidden experiments, feral children, idioglossia, invented sign language, and pidgin/creole and hybrid language varieties. These are classic areas of interest in investigations into the origin and nature of human language and the creation of new languages. Yet significant aspects of Colin and Sadiki's experiences are absent from these discussions. Looking through this wide array of overlapping interdisciplinary theoretical and analytic lenses, the expansive nature and broad scope of the research still seem to limit, obscure, and marginalize many key behaviors, emotions, and influences that filled Sadiki and Colin's everyday life experiences. Many of the underlying research paradigms have a heavy focus on deprivation, experimentation, and an almost exclusive emphasis on the

Kisisi (Our Language): The Story of Colin and Sadiki, First Edition. Perry Gilmore.
© 2016 Perry Gilmore. Published 2016 by John Wiley & Sons, Inc.

forms and structural features of language. Most of these well-known language origin studies fail to consider the ethnographic dimensions of the unique cultural contexts in which the new languages occur and the meanings these languages hold not only for the participants who speak them but also for those who observe them being spoken. It is also crucial to consider the "childrenness"[3] of these phenomena which is often hard to find in language origin studies. Absent are the playful aspects of the children's exchanges – the fun, the fantasy, the giggles, the joyful intensity, the delightful mischievousness, and the close bonds of friendship that fill the lives of young children. Also missing in these studies is the recognition of children's dramatic virtuosity in their artistic verbal performances and in their aesthetic creative processes – the emotive, aesthetic, and literary functions of language, what Jacobson[4] identifies as poetics. Where are the playful, humorous, creative, and aesthetic aspects of child language innovation?

In my experience I have found that folklorists have frequently been the scholars who have most highlighted the richest conceptualization of children's authentic expressive behaviors and situated communication. Many folklore studies focus specifically on children's speech play and verbal art: the whimsical, playful, and artful aspects of children's spontaneous language use and folklore.[5] The Russian folklorist, children's poet, and literary critic Kornei Chukovsky[6] is well known for his expressed wonder and delight in children's language creativity and ingenuity, identifying them as "linguistic geniuses" and "tireless explorers." He writes, "Enchanting children's speech! It will never cease to give me joy."[7] Chukovsky's work, based on his own and others' direct observations, captured and described numerous examples of children's linguistic and cognitive creativity, their language play, and their poetic uses of language.

Also significant, folklorists do not shun but instead often study the "aggressive, obscene, scatological, anti-authoritarian, and inversive elements"[8] so prevalent in children's verbal acts and play behavior, and so often part of the fun. Many can recall the mischievous delight in secretly uttering the naughty words, song lyrics, and rhymes that we learned from our peers and not our parents. Colin and Sadiki indulged in their fair share of scatological language invention. They created an expansive and delightful lexicon for scatological artifacts and activities, including new words for urinating, defecating, and farting, in their otherwise rather restricted pidgin with its limited lexicon. Further, these vivid elaborated additions to their toilet lexicon marked detailed distinctions that did not exist in the dominant source language, Up-Country Swahili.

Folklorists try to avoid what Bauman[9] identifies as an adultocentric bias, instead seeking to understand children from their own point of view, even when that view focuses on toilet humor. I have always been drawn to ethnographic and folkloristic approaches to the study of children, language, and learning. As a children's fiction writer, it was a valuable way to understand and connect with my young readers. Later, when I was back at the University of Pennsylvania, I conducted ethnographic studies of children's language competencies, creative verbal expression, *sub rosa* literacy, play and peer culture, and the like.[10] During that time, I recall driving Colin and about a half dozen nine-year-old boys home from soccer practice one afternoon. There was loud whispering and giggling in the crowded back seat of the station wagon. Colin's voice sounded out over the hush: "You don't have to whisper, my mom studies that kinda stuff!" I did in fact always love to study things that Colin led me to – toilet humor and all. I loved watching him grow and loved what he taught me about children, play, performance, and creativity.

As Sadiki's mother, Laiton, and I stood watching our children playing together one afternoon, Laiton observed, "*Kucheza kazi ya watoto*" ("To play is the work of children"). Much work was in fact accomplished by the children through their playful acts. Sadiki and Colin's play served as a space and a resource for the inventive verbal activities that generated their shared language. The children did not make a serious joint decision to sit down to plan and develop a lexicon, organize a dictionary, or establish a set of grammatical rules. Their creative language work was not deliberately conceived but spontaneously generated in their play and in their play-related activities.

Jourdan[11] identifies the *culture of work* in slave-generated plantation pidgins as the locus for the exploration of meaning and as the social context for extended and sustained contact among the speakers. Similarly, what I might call the *culture of play* served as the interactional center for exploring meaning and the social context for Colin and Sadiki's sustained contact. Play was their place of encounter and their space for language creativity and complex linguistic innovation.

Not only was play a place to create language but language was also a place to create play. The language itself served as a space and place for play. Their focus in language play was often for its own sake and stressed the poetic and aesthetic form of the message.[12] Children typically enjoy using language as a resource for play, manipulating all of its dimensions, including sound, meaning, syntax, and lexicon, for the sake of doing just that.[13] Fascination with phonological elements of language continues far beyond the acquisition of proficiency with sound. Children play with sounds and noises and controlled articulation of rasping, devoicing, nasalization, constriction, etc. They enjoy motor noises for which cars, bombs, airplanes, and the like are given elaborate sound effects.[14]

Colin and Sadiki engaged in long and continuous hours of such verbal play where the shape of the communicative message became the central focus of attention, exploited for its own sake.[15] Due to their initial communicative limitations with one another, the children seemed to rely even more heavily on sound play and repetition in their early conversational exchanges. Before arriving at Kekopey, Colin had often been engaged in complex and lengthy narrative role play when playing with his friends back in Philadelphia. That narrative play contrasted dramatically with his initial play with Sadiki in the early months of their friendship when much of their play activities was made up of elaborate and often explosive sound effects, including crashing sounds, speeding sounds, gun sounds, machine sounds (e.g., cars, trucks, and helicopters), and the like. These sounds were mapped onto their ongoing actions with play props such as match box cars, action figures, or various small rocks and twigs that represented a range of rotating animals, vehicles, and characters.

I was well aware of their increased amount of sound play in their early interactions, especially because these creative, uniquely shaped phonological utterances presented an extremely challenging task for me as I attempted to transcribe them. I couldn't in many cases even reproduce them orally. The children appeared to have pragmatically regressed, returning to an earlier stage of language development where their verbal play and alternating repetition with sounds were more typical of two and three year olds. This simple sound play was not only fun it also provided the base from which they could move forward together, sharing the same symmetrical verbal repertoire. Not surprisingly, many of their newly invented lexical items drew on sound play and onomatopoeia. Sadiki and Colin's sound play clearly provided a fertile resource for the creation of many of the newly created words, or neologisms, in their language.

In one case, Colin was not only able to provide me with the translation but also with an etymology for one of these onomatopoetic invented words. Colin was my primary interpreter, especially in those early months when my own Swahili was not yet good enough to ask Sadiki for his interpretations. I had been recording the boys regularly in the first weeks of my discovery of their language. I was trying to translate and make sense of one of my early transcripts. The boys had uttered the phrase *naenda diding*. I knew the expression *naenda* meant *go* (*na-* being the present tense marker for the verb *go*) in Swahili. But I did not know the word *diding*. I asked Colin to translate for me. Without hesitating, he told me that it meant "fast." Then, without any prompting, he began to tell me the story of how the word actually came to be. He explained that one day, soon after we had arrived, Sadiki and he were outside kicking a soccer ball back and forth. This had become a favorite part of their daily play ritual. All was fine until Colin looked up and saw the entire baboon troop, just a few hundred feet away, coming up over the cliff and toward them. The Pumphouse Gang baboons were known hunters and predators[16] and took down gazelles and other prey larger than the children. The rule was that when the baboons came anywhere near the headquarters, the boys had to be inside with all of the windows and doors locked. Colin knew that he had to act quickly. Sadiki could not see the baboons coming up behind him and Colin said that he could not remember the Swahili word for "fast." He explained that in that moment of panic and urgency, he shouted out the familiar play noise the two boys often made to represent the sound of speeding cars and planes. *"Diding! Diding!"* It seemed that Sadiki immediately understood. They both ran fast and safely entered the headquarters.

Diding, originally articulated with more nasalized, explosive, and rasping sounds, was gradually phonologically modified to follow the Kisisi sound system, which for the most part largely mirrored the phonological rules of Up-Country Swahili. The word took on its new semantic value and was officially added to their lexical repertoire. Like many of their invented words or neologisms, *diding* originated in sound play and onomatopoeia and is an excellent illustration of how their artful verbal play and repetition were crucial discourse devices for lexical invention. It is also a striking example of how the poetic elements of language contribute to meaning making. A creative sound, explored, manipulated, and played with repeatedly by both children, modifies its phonological shape, acquires a semantic value, and becomes a new vocabulary word, or lexical item.

I thanked Colin and turned back to my transcribing, jotting down as best as I could remember his vivid and animated narration of this dramatic word history. He remained at my desk looking over my shoulder for a few more minutes. Then, as he turned to walk away, he offhandedly commented, "You didn't spell it right." When I asked what he meant, he answered, "Because our language has sounds that aren't in the alphabet." This display of metalinguistic awareness, being so conscious of and so articulate about the language and specific linguistic behaviors, surprised me almost as much as their lexical invention did. Not only was he able to recount a detailed etymological history of a single lexical item, but further he could speculate about its complex rules for a Kisisi orthography and the implications for Kisisi literacy. At this time, he was only five and a half and just a novice writer himself. But he knew enough about the alphabet to know that these sounds didn't match.

The neologism *diding* was invented through sound play in the first few weeks of the boys' time together. Nearly 15 months later, invented by the children four days before we left Kenya, the next example presents the neologism *pupu*. This newly invented word similarly grew out of the children's verbal sound play exchanges. Instead of being told the history of the invention of *pupu*, I happened to serendipitously capture its evolution on a tape recording. The following transcript and analysis present a "close-up" processual look at a discursive interaction depicting the actual birth of the lexical item and providing a detailed and dynamic examination of the boys' creative imagination, sound play, and fun within their ongoing conversation. The recordings and transcribed data detailed many such verbal exchanges in which the boys demonstrate their metalinguistic awareness and metapragmatic competence. They often refined, defined, negotiated, and discussed new lexical items or negotiated meaning in syntactic (mis)communications. Their new word invention and lexical stock were continually growing until the time we left Kenya and the two children were separated. There is some indication that more mutually known English words were being incorporated as time went by and Sadiki's English became more competent, especially after they started going to school together. Yet new word invention in their pidgin continued until the end. On one of the last recordings I made before we left Kenya, the genesis of the word *pupu*, embedded in ongoing and fluid conversational exchanges, was unexpectedly captured while the boys were having tea (*chai*) and eating freshly baked breads that they had helped me prepare earlier.

The bread was my favorite, an old Philadelphia Quaker Meeting bread recipe, borrowed originally from the Finnish sweet bread called *pulla*. Joab called this my *mkate ya sukari* (sugar bread) and it was something Joab and I agreed that I would regularly prepare in our kitchen. It was great with tea and Joab enjoyed it too. The sweet dough, meant to be braided, is so flexible that the children could shape it easily, like clay, into wonderful creative forms of trucks, cars, tractors, and the like. I had just removed the bread from our large, pale green Dover woodstove and the sweet aroma filled the air.

The transcript below presents the discourse surrounding the actual creation of the boys' new lexical item as it was shaped, formed, negotiated, and agreed upon. Like the bread they were eating, this too was a new form they had made together and shared. The newly invented word, *pupu*, not too surprisingly, meant *fart*. The slightly pejorative meaning and onomatopoeic aspects no doubt made this word particularly delightful, naughty, and appealing to and representative of the children and their play with scatological words and toilet topics.

For example, *dudu* is the Swahili word for a large insect. One of the visitors who came to the headquarters was an entomologist who enlisted the children to help him collect insect samples with a net he provided. They delighted in calling him *Bwana Dudu* (Mister Bug), which made them laugh each time they said his name. Certainly, Colin knew the English scatological meaning of the word *dudu,* and I assume he shared the *double entendre* with Sadiki.

There may be a possibility that the word *pooh* or something similar was known to Colin in English. I do not recall his ever using it and at this time he had been in Africa for more than a year. I believe it was a new word and not an English loan word, although the influence of similar words in English (e.g., *poop, poos*) was no doubt operating. William Samarin, in a personal letter,[17] offered a different explanation for the meaning and origin of *pupu,* tracing the word to Sango origins, where *pupu* means wind, and suggesting that Colin may have heard the word and "stored the phonological shape and some of its semantics" and later extended its meaning. Since no one anywhere near the hill spoke Sango, I didn't agree with his conclusion. However, I found the possible alternative lexical histories fascinating and appreciated his interest.

As demonstrated in the transcript below, the process of lexical innovation flows slowly and persistently through, and is embedded in, the rhythmic context of their ongoing playful interactions and conversational exchanges. A discourse analysis of these data provides a close look at and details their playful language creativity – the generative, meaning-making, and metalinguistic discursive processes. I have bolded the development of the word from its initial sound to ultimate lexical shape to help the reader and mark its flow through the discourse.

The children are drinking tea and eating the freshly baked breads they made in the shape of tires, tractors, and balls. Colin's father (F) sits with them at the table.

[x = inaudible syllable]

1. Colin:	xx na kula. Silly. Silly I. Silly hello. Sema Sadiki "hello" las ingine.	
	(xx eat. Silly. Silly I. Silly hello. Sadiki say more like this "hello".)	
2. Sadiki:	Silly bottom. (laughs) **Pzzzt**.	
	[Sadiki makes a "farting" sound]	
3. Colin:	Bottom fanya nini?	
	(Bottom makes what?)	
4. Sadiki:	Bottom nafanya **pzzzt**.	
	(Bottom makes pzzzt.)	

5. Colin:	Nafanya **paauu**
	make paau
	(It makes paauu.)

6. Sadiki:	Ach! Mimi nataka thas mingi. Wewe nataka? Uh-huh?
	Ach! me want this many you want yes
	(Ach! I want lots of these. Do you want [some]? Yes?)

7. Colin:	Mimi ndiyo.
	me yes
	(Yes, I do.)

| 8. Sadiki: | Uh? |

9. Colin:	Mimi kubwa tire. [loud comic voice and holding up a big bread]
	me big tire
	(My big tire.)

| 10. Sadiki: | (laughs) |

11. Colin:	Mimi hakuna taka kula mimi tire.
	me no want eat me tire
	(I don't want to eat my tire.)

| 12. Sadiki: | Huh? (laughing) |

13. Colin:	Mimi hakuna taka kula moja kubwa tire. [loud comic voice]
	me no want eat one big tire
	(I don't want to eat the big tire.)

| 14. Sadiki: | xxx? |
| | [F takes some of the bread] |

| 15. Colin: | (to F) That's Sadiki's ... bread. That bread. |

16. (to Sadiki):	Tegid wewe mkate.
	take it you bread
	(He took your bread.)

| 17. F: | Hii mkate yango. [teasingly in Swahili to both children] |
| | (This is my bread.) |

18. Colin:	(to F) Umum. Mkate kwa mimi.
	no bread for me
	(No. The bread is for me.)

| 19. Sadiki: | (to F) Kula thas mimi mkate kwa Colin, yeh? |

eat this me bread for Colin yeh
(Eat my bread instead of Colin's, yes?)
[F puts the bread back and the boys return to talking to each other]

20. Colin: Kula thas mingi.
eat this many
(Eat lots of these.)

21. Sadiki: Kula moja tire. Mingi kubwa. Kula moja tire.
eat one tire many big eat one tire
(Eat a tire. Many are big. Eat a tire.)

22. Colin: Thas kwa **pupu** na moja kula moja tire ... xx mimi tire?
this for fart *na* one eat one tire xx me tire
(It makes you fart if you eat the tire ... xx my tire?)

23. Sadiki: Thas kwa **pupu** na moja kula moja tire ... xx mimi tire?
[Repeats Colin's utterance exactly with precise prosody and intonation]
(It makes you fart if you eat the tire ... xx my tire?)

24. Colin: Huh?

25. Sadiki: (laughs)

26. Colin: Nini we lathas? Nafanya nini? [looking at one of Sadiki's breads]
what you like this make what
(What did you make like this? What did you make?)

27. Sadiki: xxx nakula mimi mkate? [Talks with mouth full]
(xxx eat my bread?)

28. Colin: Kwa kucheza wewe nini?
for play you what
(Who will you be for play/pretend?)

29. Sadiki: Oge? xx bandit
(Okay? xx bandit)

30. Colin: Kwa kucheza mi xx bandit.
(For play I'll be a bandit.)

31. Sadiki: xxx

32. Colin: Wewe jua nini **pupu**?
you know what <u>pupu</u>

(Do you know what <u>pupu</u> is?)

33. Sadiki: **Pupu?** [laughing] xx **pupu?** [laughing]

34. Colin: Uh uh, **pupu** ... **pupu** moja thas, wewe na sidown kwa
choo,
moja **pupu's** cumin.
no pupu pupu one this you sit down for bowel movement
one pupu's coming
(No, pupu ... pupu is this, when you sit down for a
bowel
movement a pupu is coming.)

35. Sadiki: Oh. [laughs]

The full cycle of invention depicted in the above transcript includes several distinct characteristic elements that are possibly typical of the etymologies of many neologisms in the pidgin (e.g., *kiki/break*, *tena/fast*, *diding/very fast*, *gninginge/speeding*). These elements include: (1) onomatopoeia and sound play (line 2: **pzzzt**), (2) designation of a semantic value to the sound play vocalization (line 4: Bottom **nafanya pzzzt**), and (3) adaptation of the play sound to the phonological system with eventual reduplication (lines 2, 4: **pzzzt** > line 5: **paauu** > line 22, 23, 32–35: **pupu**). Others[18] have noted similar speculations about individual children creating lexical items in these ways, the way a child might come to call a truck a *vroom*.

The three characteristics mentioned above function quite independently of any joint discourse effort or conversation. But as the text above illustrates, this particular progression from playful sound to lexical item occurs gradually and is woven through and integrated into the flow of their discursive interactions. When a shared and symmetrical language is developed (as opposed to an individual child's lexical innovation), an additional set of interactive elements must be operating as well. The text illustrates several such discourse devices used for mutually understanding these linguistic inventions. This cooperative process includes (1) repetition (lines 23, 33), (2) definition (line 34), and (3) agreement (lines 5, 35). These characteristics provide the communicative resources for developing the shared competence in their emerging language.

Consider further analysis of the discursive processual interaction. In line 1, Colin appears to be inviting Sadiki to join him in his verbal play with the word *silly*. Sadiki responds to the game saying *silly bottom* (line 2), a frequent Britishism used teasingly by and with their schoolmates. Sadiki then adds the farting sound. Instead of continuing the play with *silly*, Colin, proba- bly amused by Sadiki's little off-color joke, responds to Sadiki and asks the question in line 14, *Bottom fanya ninyi?* The conversation then briefly focuses on the designation of shared meaning for the sound *pzzzt*. It is possible at this point that Colin may have wanted to stay with this topic and initiate the lexical agreement he seems to be moving toward. But Sadiki changes the topic and they both move on. When the lexical item *pupu* first appears in line 22, it suggests that Colin has not dropped his original interest and has in fact been modifying the phonological shape of the original sound to fit the Kisisi phonological system. Sadiki's immediate and exact imitation and repetition (line 23) in response to Colin's utterance is the only such response in this protocol. Sadiki repeats the utterance with the exact into- nation and prosody. His precise repetition of the utterance appears to be a spontaneous reaction to the fact that he did *not* understand what Colin said, possibly because of the inclusion of the new lexical item *pupu*. At this point in the interaction, there is no reason to guess that Sadiki recognized *pupu* as a word. The repetition performed the function of at least briefly keep- ing the conversation going[19] and allowing Sadiki the chance to play with and duplicate the unknown sound and utterance. In developing a shared language, repetitions of new vocalizations are probably essential to produce equally competent speakers.

In line 32 when Colin directly asks Sadiki if he knows what *pupu* means, the conversation moves to a metalinguistic level, where the children can objectify, reflect on, and use language to discuss and expand their own lan- guage. Sadiki laughs and says "Oh," seeming to indicate he understands, accepts, and is amused. The process of defining and agreeing is not uncon- sciously evolving through sound play and repetitions but is in this particular instance an articulated negotiation, acknowledging the arbitrary nature of language. This ability to agree on and discuss their language in this way is another device for ensuring the shared competence and symmetrical per- formance of their pidgin.

Sutton-Smith[20] has suggested that play and fantasy provide a place where an overabundance of ideas is generated which may later be used and adapted for other purposes. In Kisisi, this was the case as verbal play brought about linguistic invention and mutual agreement, as illustrated in the examples of *diding* and *pupu*. Play with language was not only a source of lexical creativity but of grammatical innovation as well. (More detailed examples of their playful lexical and complex syntactic linguistic creativity will be further explored in Chapter 5.)

Ochs Keenan[21] has demonstrated that repetition, so predominant in early language and verbal play, can perform a wide variety of functions in conversation, including agreeing, self-informing, displaying knowledge, and generally keeping the discourse going. Kisisi offers further examples of the function of repetition. In the case of Kisisi, repetition in verbal play became a means of teaching and learning together, a strategy for sharing. For Colin and Sadiki, repetitions were a way of agreeing, memorizing, and building a shared dictionary and set of grammatical rules. Playful repetitions ensured the symmetrical performance of the language by both children. This is demonstrated in line 23 of the *pupu* transcript above, when Sadiki repeats Colin's utterance exactly, apparently a strategy to keep the conversation going in spite of his not understanding. Indeed, as I continued to analyze their language data, I was almost surprised to find the consistent degree of striking symmetry in their ongoing verbal performances at all stages of their language development across the 15 months. They were continuously ensuring shared proficiency through playful acts of repetition, continuous turn-taking verbal interaction, and regular metalinguistic discursive negotiations.

Play has often been explained as merely a preparation for adult life, practice for the future. The play that created Kisisi seems by that definition to be wasted energy. It was not aimed at accomplishing acculturation into the adult language and community. Instead, it was aimed at the creation of a new language and a new community, a child community, a separate speech community for two. Their demonstrations of creative competence are examples of the valuable insights into the development of communicative competence that can be found in the study of improvised spontaneous speech play used by all children. Their language creation is also a form of the inversive mischief and anti-authoritarian resistance so characteristic of children's speech play and folklore. Part of the delight with using a secret language is in fact because it is secret – secret from authority figures, including parents and teachers.

Cremin and Maybin note that children's language creativity can "provide a space for subversion, resistance and critique, for instance through breaking taboos, or providing radical commentary."[22] Beyond delightfully "naughty" taboo words, Colin and Sadiki's performative verbal activity also provided the vehicle for the strong social agency that the children were able to exercise when they resisted the postcolonial racialized hegemonic ideologies, biased attitudes and negative behaviors that surrounded them by boldly and fearlessly speaking their own language – a private language, regularly displayed in public performances and conveying a strong symbolic message. (Evidence of and discussions about the boys' social awareness, resistant agency, and enacted language ideologies will be more deeply explored in Chapter 4.)

It has been said by Chukovsky that "only those ideas can become toys for him whose proper relation to reality is firmly known to him."[23] It can be suggested, therefore, that the kinds of manipulation of language at all levels from morphophonemic to sociolinguistic that were accomplished by the two speakers of Kisisi provide insight into the transformational psychological, political, and cultural realities of the linguistic structural and stylistic elements "played with." Shatz and Gelman[24] in their research demonstrated that four year olds can appropriately simplify their speech when talking to two year olds. The case of the boys' spontaneous pidgin suggests that the same simplification metric was employed when the two children came into contact. This process would account for the ability of young children to originate (as opposed to learn) a novel simplified register, an original pidgin. But what accounts for the expansion, elaboration, and complication process that is also very apparent in the language? The example Kisisi offers suggests that linguistic playfulness and creativity, characteristic of children's verbal performance, contribute the momentum for the elaborative creolization process.

Jakobson[25] has noted that the poetic function of children's speech play displays manipulation for its own sake. Features common to the interactions between Colin and Sadiki, such as alliteration, repetition, rhyme, metaphor, and imagery, are illustrative of linguistic expressiveness.[26] An illustration of this type of metaphoric creativity can be seen in the modification of several Swahili loan words the boys combined to create new meanings. This process of calquing, or compounding, generated poetic imagery and lexical invention. For example, the word for sun in Swahili is *jua*. Compounding two Swahili words, the boys instead called the sun *kubwa moto* or big fire, displaying their rich metaphoric inventiveness. The word for train is *traini* in Swahili. The boys' Kisisi word for train was *motoga* (car) *moto* (fire). In their word for train, *moto* (the word for fire) is not a ball of fire as depicted in the word for the sun, but a "fired up" engine that distinguishes a train from a car. The word *choo* in Swahili has multiple meanings – it can refer to feces, urine, or the lavatory itself. As mentioned above, the boys elaborated and expanded their "toilet" lexicon. For example, by compounding the Swahili word for water (*maji*) with *choo* (feces), they distinguished urinating, *maji choo*, from defecating, *choo*. In Up-Country Swahili, the word *choo* was an example of polysemy common in pidgins, where one word has more than one meaning. Sadiki and Colin elaborated that limiting restriction and distinguished various toilet functions by using metaphoric compounded Swahili loan words. Metaphoric and poetic creative language features can provide fertile ground for significant language invention as well as language development. In discussing language variants and anti-languages that are performed by subcultures to deliberately exclude outsiders (e.g., Cockney rhyming slang, thieves' cant), Halliday points out the use of metaphors at every level of language innovation from phonological, lexical, morphological, semantic, and syntactic. He states that "this metaphorical quality appears all the way up and down the system."[27]

The famous chimpanzee Washoe, in a project designed and implemented by Allen and Beatrix Gardner at the University of Nevada, was the first nonhuman primate to learn American Sign Language (ASL). Washoe combined signs for *water* and *bird* to represent a swan when she did not know the ASL sign for a swan. Koko, the well-known sign-using gorilla trained by Francine "Penny" Patterson, similarly creatively combined the signs for *bottle* and *match* to represent a cigarette lighter. These inventive nonhuman primate language behaviors are quite similar to the imagery employed in Colin and Sadiki's original compounds. These kinds of compounds are commonly used in human language innovation and language contact situations. These examples are offered here not to diminish human verbal creativity, but to note and highlight nonhuman primates' metaphoric communicative competencies, suggesting its very basic place in communication and language origins.

Feldman, Goldin-Meadow, and Gleitman[28] studied the invention of "home sign" language of deaf children to gain further understanding of the child's contribution to language learning drawing from his or her own resources. The case of Kisisi provides concrete examples and additional insight into the active contribution the child makes in the language "learning" process. Such phenomena suggest that we view all language learning as inseparable from language invention.[29]

Steven Pinker, commenting on the case of Nicaraguan Sign Language invention, states, "[This] shows that children have sophisticated mechanisms of language analysis which give language many of its distinctive qualities." He goes on to say that the Nicaraguan study shows the creative contribution of children to language by documenting "a case in which the language children end up with is *more complex* than the language they hear."[30] As the examples above demonstrate, this is also the case in Kisisi. These studies offer concrete examples of what children bring to the creation of new languages and new language varieties.

Colin and Sadiki's language is also reminiscent of the secret play languages, like Pig Latin, that children often use following rules of simple substitution and rearrangement of their shared lexicon.[31] The invention of Kisisi, however, is a very different speech phenomenon, involving extensive lexical, semantic, syntactic, and pragmatic language innovation and creativity by speakers of two different languages. Though Kisisi is clearly not a simple language game or disguised speech code, it does perform a similar function for its speakers. It is secret. It is mischievous. And it is fun. The children's pidgin set up and maintained boundaries[32] around their tiny speech community just as play languages do.

The following interaction illustrates the boys' delight in their being in the know while others are not. In this case, the outsider is Colin's father, who is recording the boys while they are swinging on a rope swing. They each take turns as they run, grab the rope, and swing high back and forth three times before jumping off. Colin and Sadiki, in chorus, count off each swing, "*Moja, mbili, tatu*" (One, two, three). A number is chanted out with each single swing. Colin is wearing Wellington rubber boots that, to his delight, keep flying off his feet and falling to the ground as he swings up in the air. Colin and Sadiki engage in playful discourse as they swing. Colin makes a statement in Kisisi (line 2 below) that is unintelligible to Colin's father, who tries to understand what Colin has just said.

1. Colin and Sadiki:	Moja, mbili, tatu. One, two, three. [Colin's boot falls off]
2. Colin:	Ende mimi boot nawenda kiki sasa na kuja. Hakuna mbaya! go me boot goes broke now and come not bad (My boot keeps on falling off. It's not bad!)
3. Father:	What did you say, Colin?
4. Sadiki:	Wewe na boot nawenda ki. you na boot go broke (Your boot fell off.)
5. Colin:	Sema kwa mimi boot. [answering his father] say about me boot (I'm talking about my boot.)
6. Father:	Huh?
7. Colin:	Mimi sema kwa mimi boot. me say about me boot (I'm talking about my boot.)
8. Colin and Sadiki:	Moja, mbili, tatu. [Sadiki swings] One, two, three.
9. Father:	What's that mean? [asking Colin what he had said]

10. Colin:	What mean?
11. Father:	What you said about your boots.
12. Colin:	Mimi boot nawenda. My boot ran away, Silly!
	me boot goes my boot ran away, silly
	(My boot goes. My boot ran away, Silly!)
13. Sadiki:	[laughs]
14. Colin:	Bwana Hugh hakuna ju nini. [to Sadiki]
	Bwana Hugh nothing knows what
	(mister Hugh doesn't know anything.)

Kisisi is secret and it is fun. It is an in-group language shared by the boys and no one else. Hugh is baffled (line 3) by Colin's unintelligible utterance (line 2) about his boot. Colin uses numerous novel Kisisi grammatical devices to indicate that his boots are repeatedly falling off. None of these linguistic devices are used in Up-Country Swahili and therefore were not understood by Colin's father. Sadiki indicates his own understanding when he paraphrases Colin's utterance in line 4. He may also have been repeating that simplified paraphrase for Colin's father whom he realizes hasn't understood.

For example, Colin repeats the verb *enda* (*enda* [go] and its variation with the present tense marker *na-, nawenda*) twice, before and after the word *boot*. This is a strategy in Kisisi to show repetitive action. When something happens over and over again, the verb is repeated to mark that iterativity. He also uses the Kisisi phrase *sasa na kuja* (now and come). Though these are all Swahili words, they are used in a way that is original, marked, and mean something new. The phrase *sasa na kuja* is another device to indicate that the boot fell off now and it will again in the coming near future – another way to note iterative, repeated, or habitual action. The verb *ki* or *kiki* is a Kisisi neologism that means *to break* or *broken*. The novel word appears to have originated in sound play, resembling a crashing sound. (The English word *crash* itself has onomatopoeic qualities.) *Kiki* follows the verb *nawenda* (go) to emphasize duration of the action of breaking. Colin translates that idea loosely, humorously, and metaphorically when he tells his father that the boot ran away (line 12). Even when the children know that we have become interested in their private language and that they are being recorded, they still enjoy their in-group solidarity. In the interaction above, Colin (line 14) seems to delight in telling Sadiki that his father "doesn't know anything." While Colin offers translations in response to his father's requests, he marks Kisisi's boundaries by calling his father "silly" (line 12) for not knowing.

Colin's calling his father "silly" is something that Sadiki would never say to his father or any other adult. These playful discursive practices of Colin's, while they may have been amusing to and tolerated by us, were no doubt outrageous to Sadiki, who simply laughs at his friend in line 13. (See Chapter 5 for further discussion of their lexical and syntactic innovations and their original linguistic devices for expressing time, tense and aspect.)

Mukarovsky,[33] the Czech literary and aesthetic theorist associated with the Prague Linguistic Circle, has emphasized the aesthetic value of language, noting that linguistic features, art, and communication are all intricately related and their borders are often crossed. Cremin and Maybin, in a discussion of children's language creativity, note that vernacular creativity in the everyday spoken language of ordinary people is of increasing interest to scholars who explore the poetic, narrative, and performative aspects of the artful uses of everyday language, especially focusing on the dynamic "processes of improvisation, adaptation and transformation."[34]

The boys' special language crossed, transgressed, and transcended the marked social and linguistic borders of hegemonic postcolonial Kenya. They were bold and public in their discursive performances of their private language. They also thrived on the positive support everyone on the hillside offered. The boys' resistance to the prevailing language ideologies that established inequality among speakers[35] was multilayered and paradoxical. According to the prevailing postcolonial language practices, these two children – one black, one white – were expected to use the local Up-Country Swahili when speaking to each other, if indeed they spoke together at all. Interactions between white and African children were not really accepted, especially when they crossed not only racial lines but also lines of economics, education, and class. There was a small African elite population, but certainly Sadiki did not belong to that. A close cross-racial friendship like theirs was an uncommon and bold exception.

Our host and Kekopey owner, Tobina Cole, in an interview in 2010, reflecting on her family experiences in Kenya, described growing up "English" in Kenya in the colonial era meant that "you wore white socks and didn't speak to Africans."[36] In the postcolonial period after Kenya's independence from British rule, most white Kenyan children were still strongly discouraged from speaking to Africans at all.

Colin and Sadiki's close relationship was shocking to many of the local British expatriates. Their Kisisi language performances disturbed, interrupted, and transformed the existing symbolic social order by semiotically pronouncing a very different social equation about their relationship to each other and to the surrounding community. While the larger colonial language practices and social order prevailed, the smaller hillside community had from the start of the discovery of Kisisi made it clear that the boys' special language was a "blessing" and a "gift from God (*Mungu*)." My own research interest in and regular tape recordings of their language also added to its elevated status and legitimacy on the hill. Their language came to function as a kind of symbolic capital[37] for the children, establishing a value in their relationship and reinforcing the recognition, acceptance, increased prestige, and elevated status of their friendship. Their resistance therefore might be considered a sanctioned resistance, one in which their free, bold, and risk-taking "fearless speech"[38] and newly performed aligned identity and presentation of self[39] were not thwarted in their immediate social context. The situation may have unfolded very differently if, for example, I had forbidden them to use the language because I feared it might interfere with their language development, or if Sadiki's family felt it violated their own cultural norms.

Instead, their language functioned as what linguistic anthropologist Alexandra Jaffe might describe as a stance-saturated linguistic form used to challenge "social, political and moral hierarchies."[40] When called on to translate for each other in public, for example, the two would stand up very close, faces almost touching, and whisper in Kisisi. These ritualized public translations of their private language were theatrical and dramatic verbal performances displayed, for example, when English- or Swahili-speaking children came to visit. These speech events usually involved directions for soccer games, races, and the like. Whether in all cases they needed one another to translate is unclear, especially as time went on and they each had acquired more language competencies in English (for Sadiki) and Swahili (for Colin). Nonetheless, the ritual of translation – both a public and private performance at once – persisted to the end. The performances of these identity rituals were a way for them to "give off"[41] information; a metamessage about who they were, and the establishment of boundary markers to the others present.[42] Their pidgin language not only facilitated their communication but made a social semiotic statement about the existence of, and the values and beliefs in, their own speech community. Their own language ideology was a metapragmatic[43] pronouncement. It was a public declaration of the symmetry of their relationship. It was a public display of their strong belief in the possibility that the existing rigid and oppressive biases of the everyday language policies and practices surrounding them could be challenged and transgressed by two young, bold, border-crossing friends.

Identities may be chosen and/or imposed by language use – used to distance and differentiate or for creating shared identities. Mary Bucholtz describes identity reconstruction through language use as "emerg[ing] over time through discursive and other social practices."[44] She suggests that identity is produced in social interaction and through a process of contestation and collaboration. Sadiki and Colin created new identities and initiated new rule-changing everyday local language practices and policies[45] enacted through their own talk.

Often their dramatic narrative role play was also a window into their underlying ideologies, their collective beliefs and values, and the shared reality they constructed and reinforced daily through their enacted dramatic role playing and artful verbal performances. One poignant and powerful narrative was frequently enacted and strikingly captured their strong beliefs and values. They regularly and repeatedly role played a basic narrative sequence which they dramatized with the small figurines and match box car collection Colin had brought with him from the States. They would generally identify themselves as the heroes, Batman and Action Man. These were the "good guys."

As most of the Kenyan population, the children were enthusiastic followers of the well-known East African Safari Rally, where international drivers compete with special fast cars (e.g., Peugeot, Porsche, Datsun, Mercedes, Ford Escort, Mitsubishi, Volkswagen) at high speeds over challenging dirt and mud roads for long distances, long hours, and long days. The drivers and their cars were followed closely daily during the race. The children seemed never to tire of reenacting the rally with all of their accompanying magnificent, loud, and varied sound effects.

The twist of their play, which was unexpected for me, was the recurring and interwoven narrative thread of the evils of the slave trade. The "bad guys" were always the slave traders (or robbers), who were capturing and kidnapping Africans, jailing them, and sending them to America to be slaves. The events all took place in the speeding cars and in the villages along the route of the East African Safari Rally, which they frequently renamed the "Slave Safari." The "bad guys" would capture, threaten, and lock up the Africans to await the ships that would come to carry them overseas and away from their homes and families. Batman and Action Man, also driving fast cars, would eventually come to their rescue, releasing the slaves and fighting with and eventually defeating the slave traders. These rescues usually involved explosive fistfights, car crashes, and guns. The narrative dramatizations clearly expressed their knowledge and awareness of the oppressive and brutal history of Kenya and their very clear judgment of the good and bad of those events.

I don't recall any specific books we might have read to Colin or the conversations we might have had that served as the source of his knowledge. However, as an educator in the late 1960s and early 1970s, I had been deeply involved in curriculum development focused on the relatively new field of black history. Colin had certainly been exposed to that general knowledge in our home. I have no doubt that I talked about that history as we prepared to go to Kenya, but I have no clear memories of it and nothing in my journals or letters specifically mentions it. I wasn't sure what slave history Sadiki knew from his own family, but there were frequent political conversations among all of our African neighbors on the hill. Clearly, though, both children knew the history of slavery and knew that it was bad. Their "Slave Safari" narrative, always performed in Kisisi, was a poignant and powerful reminder that they were continually in the process of constructing a better world through the communicative force of their verbal art and creative discursive imaginary play. Their alternative social reality created a better place both by speaking Kisisi and by enacting a healing corrective history.

Their Kisisi language performances transfixed and transformed those around them who were touched by their bold love story. Through daily play and language creation, they both generated and were affected by these unfolding new language ideologies. The language created a place for their friendship – a place "invested with meaning" that shaped social life and served as a "critical force ... both locational and conceptual, physical and psychical."[46] This place, constructed through and by language, both held and projected their language identities and ideologies. These identities, created through their verbal art and linguistic creativity, were performed with a strong semiotic message of social critique and ideological transformation.

While ideology is often identified as explicitly discursive, it can also be seen, as in the case of Colin and Sadiki, as behavioral, structural, inexplicit, pre-reflective, and unconscious signifying language practices to be observed in lived experience.[47] Though their language ideologies were not often explicitly discursive, they were regularly, powerfully, and symbolically enacted. Their language, unintelligible to everyone else, markedly changed the linguistic ecology of their tiny hillside community and in some small but significant ways affected the language ideologies, practices, and policies of every other child and adult living and visiting there.

Sadiki and Colin created Kisisi, in large part, through their discursive play and expressive verbal art, drawing on their own developmental language competencies and on the range of language resources immediately available to them in their multilingual hillside environment. These bits and pieces took new shape and form in the creation of something transformational, fresh, and novel – a marked and visible language variety where none had existed before. Claude Lévi-Strauss[48] introduced the concept of cultural *bricolage,* the improvisational process of taking up a diverse range of resources and materials that are immediately at hand in order to create something new. *Bricolage* is not a deliberate strategy of reinvention but an adaptive mode of "being in the world" that can produce something new. In the case of Kisisi, *bricolage* produced a new language variety. The relationship between a sociological understanding of creolization and *bricolage* has been described by Vergès:

> Creolization is about *bricolage* drawing freely upon what is available, recreating with new content and in new forms a distinctive culture, a creation in a situation of domination and conflict. It is not about retentions but about reinterpretations ... processes of creolization appear in zones of conflict and contact. They are the harbingers of an ongoing ethics of sharing the world.[49]

In creating Kisisi, Sadiki and Colin can be seen as social critics, playful inventors, improvisational *bricoleurs*, adaptive creolizers, and verbal artists who were inspired by what folklorist, poet, and critic Edward Hirsch describes as the "indefinable source which animates different creators and infuses their deepest efforts."[50] Many across the disciplines have speculated about the nature and essence of the creative process, but for me it is the poet Federico García Lorca who has captured the mystery of the phenomenon of the creative process most profoundly. In his classic essay *Play and Theory of the Duende*, based on a lecture he delivered in Buenos Aires in 1933, Lorca described the *duende* as the power and struggle of spontaneous creation, as a "burst of inspiration, the blush of all that is truly alive, all that the performer is creating at a certain moment."[51] Lorca writes, "The duende's arrival always means a radical change in forms. It brings to old planes unknown feelings of freshness, with the quality of something newly created, like a *miracle* (emphasis mine), and it produces an almost religious enthusiasm."[52]

I see Sadiki and Colin's language invention is a vivid example of Lorca's miracle – a creative work of verbal art and an inspiring improvisational spoken performance; it was a burst of discursive freshness that brought a radical change in language form to their little hillside. The boys' continuous and spontaneous creative play with each other, and with language, generated fresh and new verbal structures and practices. Their improvisations became new expressive forms never before heard or uttered. Their everyday ordinary language performances created a theatrical spectacle on the hillside, emotionally stirring audiences and evoking *Mungu's* (God's) presence – and an almost sacred respect, awe, and reverence.

In Lorca's original lecture, he referred to the thousand boring lectures he attended in his studies in Madrid that made him "hungry for air and sunlight" and feel "covered by a light film of ash."[53] Instead of the intellectual rationality of scholarship, he turned to the *duende* to explain the unexplainable about the art of creation. He describes the *duende* as "a mysterious power which everyone senses but no philosopher explains." [54] The *duende*, derived from the Spanish word for an elf-like figure in Spanish mythology, represents the spirit of evocation. It is a heightened state of human reality with all its joys and sorrows, of spine-chilling authenticity, and of irrational and intense emotion. The *duende*, especially associated with the evocative aesthetics of flamenco and the bullfight, has also been invoked to both inspire and explain a range of modern art forms in music, painting, and poetry.[55] The *duende* has four elements, according to Maurer: irrationality, earthiness, a dash of the diabolical, and lastly a heightened awareness of death.[56]

I see all of these elements in Colin and Sadiki's experience with language invention. Their creation was not part of intellectually skilled thought process or a rationally planned strategy, but instead it was the product of their spontaneous playful improvisations. Their full presence was in the earthiness of real life and authentic emotion, in what Lorca identified as living style. Their dash of the diabolical was evident in both their playful mischievous secrecy and in their potent resistance to the colonial legacies of racialized language ideologies, taking risks and being unafraid to boldly speak their truth – their language, Kisisi. Finally, there is the ephemeral nature of their language. From the time they met and gave birth to their language, everyone on the hillside knew that we would eventually be leaving and therefore the inevitable death of Kisisi was predictable and anticipated. The situation was known by everyone to be temporary, impermanent, and transient. Our delight and joy in being together were always intensified by that awareness. Soon after their language was discovered, Sadiki's mother, Laiton, made a beautiful deep blue and red Samburu beaded bracelet for Colin. When she gave it to me, she explained that when Colin was back in America, he should wear the bracelet and remember Sadiki. Later that year, she made him two more very special beaded wristbands. Everyone knew we were only passing neighbors and that the children's close proximity as well as their opportunities to breathe life into their blessed language would be coming to an end.

I look at those three beautiful Samburu beaded bracelets now, preserved and displayed in a glass-covered shadow box on my wall so many years later. I look at the beautiful bracelets with a heightened awareness of death; the death of their language and a time long gone by. I look at the bracelets with the ever present painful and heightened awareness of Colin's absence. I look at the bracelets and vividly remember them on Colin's small wrist as he and Sadiki ran through the tall grasses on Kekopey, joyfully laughing and chattering in Kisisi, treasuring the exquisite pleasure and ease of being together. The death of their brilliant but short-lived language is reminiscent of ephemeral sand sculptures, shaped with skill and artful inspiration, only to be swept away by the inevitable ocean tides. The use of the boys' beautiful evanescent Kisisi language vanished in the inevitable flow of life events that eventually separated its young creators across the continents.

I see Colin and Sadiki's language creation as one of Lorca's miracles, as inspirational, mysterious, and magical. I hear the *duende* in Sadiki and Colin's creative, intimate, intense, and loving language engagements and euphoric laughter on my old recordings.

The *duende* is clearly missing in the many descriptions of the forbidden experiments; it is also missing in the many other accounts of language innovation where form and structure of language dominate the descriptions and the human processes of creativity, the depth of need for social connection, and the yearning for meaningful and strong emotional expression are missing. One of the lessons we might learn from the children's friendship and their language creation might be to search for the *duende* in every discourse we study. We might also do well to invoke the *duende* in order to breathe life into our own language research so that the essence of what we are studying about child language, human communication, and the human condition isn't obscured by the "light film of ash" that covered Lorca and left him "hungry for air and sunlight" in his academic studies.

CHAPTER 4

KEKOPEY LIFE: TRANSCENDING LINGUISTIC HEGEMONIC BORDERS AND RACIALIZED POSTCOLONIAL SPACES

Stories of pidgin genesis are invariably stories of people ... whose life circumstances have set the stage, created the need, and made it possible for a new pidgin to appear. But they are also the stories of cultural contacts ... and therefore of cultural change, both radical and gradual, total and partial. And obviously, they are also stories of the power relations that are at the core of the social worlds that have fostered most of the pidgin and creole languages we know.

Jourdan[1]

Settler colonialism ... strives for the dissolution of native societies ... it erects a new colonial society on the expropriated land base ... settler colonials come to stay: invasion is a structure not an event ... Settler colonialism destroys to replace.

Wolfe[2]

No late 20th-century white woman's love of animals, especially if those animals are monkeys, can be innocent of the history of racism and colonialism ...

Haraway[3]

Kekopey Ranch was the immediate context, the language contact zone, and the social world that created both the pragmatic need and the opportunity for the genesis of Colin and Sadiki's private pidgin. Any story of their pidgin

Kisisi (Our Language): The Story of Colin and Sadiki, First Edition. Perry Gilmore
© 2016 Perry Gilmore. Published 2016 by John Wiley & Sons, Inc.

and their friendship must be seen in the context of their life on Kekopey, their immediate social world and the power relations that shaped it. To understand Kekopey life, it must be viewed through the lenses of the overt and oppressive colonial structures that were firmly in place. Colin and Sadiki were mindful of both the deeply naturalized colonial ideologies and the marked language spaces. Though to my knowledge they did not explicitly discuss them, they both overtly and subtly demonstrated their awareness of the marked racialized territories, the rules that mapped on to those spaces, and the risks that came with any transgressions of their boundaries. Their appropriate behaviors and interactions in a range of social and linguistic contexts reflected their cultural knowledge. They clearly knew the rules, behaved accordingly, and were aware of when they were either engaging on the margins or crossing the borders of these bounded spaces and colonial practices.

Two distinct and prominent layers of colonialism co-existed on Kekopey. First, and most immediately obvious, was the legacy of the European white land-owning colonial settler population, especially the British aristocrats, who purchased or, in the case of the Coles, were gifted vast parcels of prime land in what were called the White Highlands. Official British policy had set aside these valuable lands for European settlement when Kenya was still a British Protectorate in the early 1900s.[4] The climate, landscape, and high altitudes (above 5000 feet) of the White Highlands were seen as suitable for European occupation and development – for building "a new country." This colonial legacy included such characteristic elements as a settler-dominated agriculture, a large and cheap indigenous labor force, indirect government rule, racialized and ethnicized power structures, and an economy designed exclusively for the benefit of the white colonial powers. Kenya held painful histories of early forced migrations and genocide by colonial military expeditions, invasion, and the imposition of colonial political structures that wrenched diplomatic power and sovereignty from the original native autochthonous populations, and Christian missionary teachings and education that were intended to make the native population obey the colonial regime and keep them in their subordinate place.[5] The land, perceived by the settlers to be empty, unknown, unsettled, unoccupied, unclaimed, and open for settlement, was actually used seasonally by its native inhabitants, often cattle- and goat-herding pastoralists who grazed the lands intermittently or others who traditionally practiced shifting agricultural cultivation or bush fallowing. When the autochthonous peoples returned, they often found their lands had been taken and occupied by Europeans in their absence. The British also acquired much of the land militarily, removing the inhabitants and relocating them to ethnic reserves.

In some cases, this process resulted in human and animal deaths, property destruction, and crop seizure.[6] As the historian Robert Maxon notes, strict segregation practices created the White Highlands, African reserves, and residential exclusiveness in the restricted all-white towns and cities, including Nairobi.[7] Similarly, geographers Heidi Frontani and Rebecca Hewitt argue that "... such land alienation was at the heart of anti-colonial struggles."[8]

These cumulative colonial structures and restricted spaces effectively eliminated the precolonial cultures and destroyed long-held egalitarian cooperative economies that were typically characterized by fluid community boundaries and interethnic trade, small-scale wars, and marriages. These cultural foundations were replaced by large land and power losses, extreme poverty, dramatic economic disparities, and heightened interethnic competition and tensions fostered by the British colonial divide-and-rule policies and practices.[9] Settler colonialism as described by Patrick Wolfe[10] includes the organizing grammar of race with its hegemonic hierarchies and structures, contests of land for life, the elimination of the native, and a pattern of destruction of the original society for replacement of it with the new dominant colonial one.

Kekopey was built on this historical settler colonial legacy. The Coles, a widely known and prominent aristocratic family in Kenya, were considered by many in the 1970s as more enlightened colonials and were seen as "rather progressive in some of their views but uncompromisingly rigid in others."[11] For example, Glenda Riley writes:

> [During the 1930s] Lady Eleanor Cole represented the East Africa's Women's League to the Associated Countrywomen of the World, where she lobbied for funds and other aid for black Kenyans. At home in Kenya, Cole became a patron of the Nyanza Musical Society, which not only introduced Africans to European music, but encouraged the performance and composition of what she termed "purely African music."[12]

Lady Cole was said to have a greater than average respect for Africans, became a citizen of Kenya early after Independence, and expressed pleasure that her children and grandchildren continued to live in Kenya.[13] The family had a reputation for relying heavily "on the old idea of patronage"[14] rather than the more blatantly bigoted and punitive management style for which many other expatriate settlers were well known.

But in spite of these reports and actions, the Coles, operating on their own deeply held colonial biases, saw Africans as not fully capable human beings. Kekopey was built on that foundation. Frontani and Hewitt sum up the colonial ideology in the following statement:

> Colonial ideology included a belief in progress through technological improvements (technocentrism), environmental ideologies of wise land use (conservationism) and protection of wildlife and lands from people (preservationism), and social Darwinism in which the Africans were viewed as incompetent, ungrateful, primitive, brutal, childlike and inferior to Europeans.[15]

There was an unquestioned assumption that their African workers were content with their low status, limited food rations, inadequate housing, and meager wages. Many years later, Tobina Cole, the daughter-in-law of Lady Cole, in an interview for a documentary film in 2010, described her father as coming from an English feudal family and treating the Africans "much more like a pack of hounds – he loved them, looked after them, they were very well housed, well clothed, well paid ..."[16] Consider that conceptions of what either Tobina or her father meant by being "well" housed, clothed or paid are based on their settler colonial ideologies. Tobina saw herself as being more enlightened than her father and as having more respect for and appreciation of the African workers. Though she described herself as having been "brought up black," based largely on her having spent much time with her mother's cook and servants, Tobina admits that she had no comprehension of what African equality and empowerment might, could, or should look like. She recalled that she was actually shocked when, as an adult, after growing up in Kenya, she first saw an African driving a car. It never occurred to her at that time that literacy, an advanced education, or a political voice could possibly be a part of an African's aspirations, let alone his or her accomplishments.

Tobina Cole, looking back and reflecting on her family's life decades later, expressed her own self-criticism and more current point of view on the colonial presence in Kenya, saying, "We were alien anyway ... we didn't think we were, but we were ... alien. We were wrong, to be here – it's their country and they must run it their way ..."[17]

Myths of hegemonic superiority are so effectively constructed and so deeply entrenched that they become unquestioned naturalized realities. I recall a story told to me by a Gujarati friend, Kirti, who was a second-generation Kenyan. In Kenya, the three-tiered social system placed Europeans at the top. The Asian Indian population, originally brought in to work on the railroad, became the middle merchant class – sometimes called the "Jews of Africa." And at the bottom of the hierarchy were the Africans.

Kirti's father had immigrated from western India. The family held English passports and had hopes of ultimately settling in England as the pressures of "Africanization" on whites and Asians increased after Kenya's Independence. Some of Kirti's relatives had already emigrated to London and at the age of 20, for the first time, Kirti left Kenya, to visit them in England. Once off the plane at Heathrow Airport, he found himself shocked and speechless as his wide-eyed gaze took in the scene before him. With tears and laughter, he saw a sight that shook him at his essence. For the first time in his life, he saw white men carrying baggage, sweeping floors, pushing boxes, hauling garbage, and wearing uniforms that marked their status as servants to the public. Somehow the colonial myth in Kenya that white Englishmen did not do *any* menial labor had been made believable. Until that moment, he had never seen, questioned, or even imagined it.

Kekopey Ranch was steeped in Kenya's colonial history and its scandals. In 1905, Lord Delamere, one of the first and most famous and influential white British settlers in Kenya, had given this large parcel of his neighboring land, Soysambu, as a gift to his brother-in-law, Lord Galbraith Lowry Egerton Cole (1881–1929). Galbraith Cole, the son of Lowry Cole, fourth Earl of Enniskillen, born into the Ascendency, Ireland's Anglo-Irish aristocracy, was one of the most wealthy and prominent settlers in the East African Protectorate. As many of the early settlers, Galbraith had initially become captivated by the romantic aura of an untamed Africa and, as his widow later wrote, "was soon fascinated with all the problems of developing a new country; he found it much more exciting than big game shooting."[18] Galbraith named the farm "Kekopey Ranch" from the Maasai word meaning "place where green turns white," referring to the dramatic change in color from the rainy season, when the landscape turns brilliant green (Tobina described it to me when we first arrived as "so green it will hurt your eyes"), to the dry season where the surrounding diatomite turns the landscape a powdery white. Galbraith was known to have been fluent in the language of the Maasai and learned much about their herding practices.

In addition to his love of the land and the wildlife and his fascination with its people, Cole also held firm the strong and deeply entrenched sense of colonial entitlement, superiority, and privilege that was so familiar, prevalent, and destructive in colonial hegemony. Raymond Williams refers to this as a practical consciousness that supports relations of domination and subordination saturating lived identities, relationships, and common sense.[19] Such a "structure of feeling" is instantiated in quotidian life yet not necessarily apparent to settlers as a set of political propositions or as a project of dispossession. Mark Rifkin argues that this "settler common sense" allows the settler to live their hegemonic biases in these regimes of power as self-evident conditions and feelings of unquestioned givenness in the "continuing assertion and exertion of settler sovereignty."[20] This unquestioned givenness was exemplified in Kirti's experiences at Heathrow Airport where the sight of white men in service disrupted and violated his own hegemonic quotidian internalized common sense. This givenness was revealed in Frontani and Hewitt's comparative study of the ideologies of land and place held by Kikuyu and colonial settler women writing in Kenya. In analyzing the authors' texts, they found that, unlike the African women writers, none of the colonial settler women authors (one of whom was Lady Eleanor Cole) "expressed any direct concern over land alienation, the colonial system of establishing small reserves for large numbers of Kenyans, or the massive wealth disparities between the two groups."[21] Galbraith Cole was saturated with this overbearing sense of "settler common sense" that Rifkin describes as its "quotidian experiences of space" and self-righteous conceptions of "jurisdiction, occupancy and ownership."[22]

In 1911, Galbraith Cole, manifesting the worst brutality of this ideology, shot and killed a Maasai laborer on his land whom he suspected of stealing his sheep. Based on historic trial documents, Robert Maxon describes the details of his controversial trial. On May 31, 1911, "he admitted shooting an African he suspected of stealing some of his sheep and not reporting the matter to police. Despite the charge of the judge to 'confine yourselves to the evidence,' the jury of nine white men took but five minutes to acquit Cole."[23] The aftermath of the trial raised further issues of colonial British justice. The governor, Sir Percy Girouard, wrote to the Colonial Office mentioning the possibility of an appeal against the verdict but stated that he had been advised not to by legal counsel. In his telegram, Girouard also stated the rationale that "The crime is due to the prevalence of unrestrained stock theft." British officials were strongly negative in their responses stating "murder is murder" and that "a callous and unjustifiable murder" was committed and there had been a "gross miscarriage of justice." Officials at the Colonial Office were even more outraged after seeing the full report of the trial. H.F. Batterbee expressed his shock that the defense counsel "did not attempt to set up any defense and evidently relied upon the jury to acquit simply because he was a white man."[24] Based on the evidence from the trial, it was determined that Cole could be deported because he was "conducting himself so as to be dangerous to the peace and good order in East Africa …"[25] Under strong pressure from the Colonial Office to deport Cole, the pro-settler governor, after exercising much resistance, served Cole the deportation order. He was deported to German East Africa. However, soon after, his mother, the Countess of Enniskillen, pleaded his case to the British government. The decision was reversed and he returned to Kekopey.

Ngugi Wa Thiong'o,[26] in his acclaimed book *Detained: A Writer's Prison Diary*, highlights and critiques these repeated examples of British settler colonial injustice, including the Cole murder case. He summarizes the events in these words: "The African is an animal: the settler is exonerated." He goes on to make his case even more strongly, writing "But I err too in saying the African was considered an animal. In reality they loved the wild game but Africans were worse, more threatening, instinctless, unlovable, unredeemable sub-animals merely useful for their brute labour."[27]

Ngugi Wa Thiong'o[28] further addresses Galbraith Cole's murder trial directly, describing Karen Blixen's (aka Isak Dinesen, the author of *Out of Africa*) retelling of the Cole case events. Wa Thiong'o expresses his disgust with Blixen's report that Cole's determined admission to the crime was an act of moral greatness. Her description follows.

> The Judge said to Gailbraith, "It's not, you know, that we don't understand that you shot only to stop the thieves." "No," Galbraith said, "I shot to kill. I said that I would so do."
>
> "Think again, Mr. Cole," said the judge. "We are convinced that you only shot to stop them."
>
> "No, by God," Galbraith said, "I shot to kill."[29]

Wa Thiong'o describes Blixen's admiration of Cole and her account as an example of how widely praised white colonial writers "turn acts of cold-blooded murder and torture of 'these black suppliers of brute labour' into deeds of heroic grandeur."[30] Wa Thiong'o asserts that the colonial system in Kenya produced a culture of "legalized brutality, a ruling-class culture of fear, the culture of an oppressing minority desperately trying to impose total silence on a restive oppressed majority."[31] The literary celebration of this culture, in his view, can be found in Blixen's writing, where she turns "Kenya into a vast erotic dreamland in which her ... Kenyan servants ... [are] usable curs and other animals."[32] Wa Thiong'o quotes a dispatch by an early governor, Sir A.R. Hardinge, on April 5, 1897, that articulates this colonial culture of silence and fear:

> Force and the prestige which rests on the belief in force, are the only way you can do anything with those people, but once beaten and disarmed they will serve you ... These people must learn submission by bullets – it's the only school; after that you may begin more modern and humane methods of education, and if you don't do it this year you will have to do it next, so why not get it over ... In Africa to have peace you must first teach obedience, and the only tutor who impresses the lesson properly is the sword.[33]

Hardinge's settler colonial philosophy was no doubt guiding Galbraith Cole in his act of the murder of his Maasai laborer on Kekopey. Ngugi Wa Thiong'o reports the history of continuous colonial brutal acts of murder, whippings, and torture committed against Africans, stating "[These] acts of animal brutality were not cases of individual aberration but an integral part of colonial politics, philosophy and culture. Reactionary violence used to instill fear and silence was the very essence of colonial settler culture."[34] His critical analyses are hauntingly juxtaposed with all of the vivid literary descriptions of the beauty of the land and wildlife in Kenya. These strongly contrasting world views reflect conflicting ideologies of the settler and the settled, the white colonial and the autochthonos displaced African.

With these brutal events on Kekopey as a permanent legacy and backdrop, six years after the trial, in 1917, Galbraith Cole married Lady Eleanor Balfour, niece of Lord Balfour, the former British Prime Minister. They had two sons, Captain David Lowry Cole (1918–1989, later the sixth Earl of Enniskillen) and Captain Arthur Gerald Cole (1920–2005). Galbraith suffered crippling and chronically painful arthritis and as a result, to end his own suffering, he committed suicide at the age of 48 in 1929. I was told many times by Cole family members about his suicide – often recounted as a part of the romanticized legacy of his strong will, bravery, and his admirable values of colonial Kenyan self-sufficiency. However, none of the family ever mentioned or shared the events of the shooting, his murder trial, or of his deportation and return. Possibly this erasure was done, consciously or unconsciously, to soften a brutal aspect of their history in order to maintain the aura of an "enlightened" colonial family in the postcolonial adjustment to becoming settlers in an independent Kenya with an African president. It is also consistent with Hardinge's 1897 philosophy of using the brutality of "sword and bullets" initially followed by more "modern and humane methods." The Coles were known for their modern and humane approach, but it was built on this early violence and the continuous potential threat of violence.

Lady Eleanor Cole (known as Nell), Galbraith's widow, for decades ran the farm with the help of European ranch managers and long-time employed African workers, mostly Maasai, who herded the cattle traditionally, on foot, with constant close handling that in Lady Cole's words "leads to calmness and docility in the cattle which astonishes those who have only seen cattle ranches ... where herding is done on horse back or by jeep."[35]

Lady Cole handed over the farm to her son Arthur in 1956. When we arrived in 1975, Lady Cole was living in their original small cottage near the main house which was then occupied by Arthur, Tobina, and their rotating four adult children who visited or stayed there at different times. Lady

Cole's grandson Berkeley Arthur Cole (1949–; the heir presumptive, Earl of Enniskillen) was the oldest son of Arthur and Tobina and was managing the ranch with Tobina during the time we lived there.

Lady Cole described some of her very first impressions of Kekopey in her memoir *Random Recollections of a Pioneer Kenya Settler*, which was written and published in 1975, the year we arrived, and given to us as a personal gift. Lady Cole wrote of her first impressions of Galbraith and his farm when she was just a young woman in 1916:

> Galbraith's farm, Kekopey, named after the little river which runs through it, was on the east side of the Lake Elmenteita, with Lord Delamere's land and house, Soysambu, on the opposite side. Elmenteita is the smallest of the three lakes along the floor of the Rift Valley, and I think the prettiest.
>
> This part of the Rift Valley is some of the most dramatically beautiful country in Kenya – along the floor of the Rift is a string of lakes – Nakuru, Elmenteita, and Naivasha. The Mau escarpment forms the western wall and the Kinagop and Aberdare range the eastern wall, and the rims of the craters stick up rather like broken teeth from various parts of the bottom land.[36]

Kekopey's majestic open savannah was home to the Coles' prized and hearty domesticated livestock carefully developed by breeding robust Santa Gertrudis bulls from the King Ranch in Texas with local disease-resistant Boran cattle. The cattle shared the Kekopey habitat with abundant and diverse wildlife. In addition to feral baboon troops, there were herds of Thomson's gazelles, impala, and zebra as well as large light-footed eland that were as big as a cow yet able to gracefully leap over high paddock fences. There were elusive and unpredictable Cape buffalo that the Coles especially liked to hunt. Tiny dik-diks, exquisite miniature deer, with huge eyes and delicate little hoofed legs, came to nibble on the deep purple bougainvillea blossoms outside the headquarters every evening. Jackal, warthog, aard-vark, hyrax, bat-eared fox, hyena, serval cat, the occasional leopard – and 32 varieties of snakes including python, puff adder, boomslang, and spitting cobra – also made Kekopey their home. Birdlife was plentiful and varied with over 400 resident species. Lake Elmenteita (also spelled Elementaita) was famously populated with hundreds of brilliant pink flamingoes, and res-ident pelicans flew over the headquarters daily on their way back and forth to feed and roost. Hippos, which could be quite dangerous on land as well as in the water, also still populated the lake at that time and were a major concern for us when we occasionally had picnics there.

The Coles were deeply committed to wildlife conservation and made every effort to balance and maintain the wildlife on the ranch, only shooting the big cats and hyena when their cattle were threatened. It was not a surprise that Kekopey had been a favored place for the many royals and distinguished international guests (including, I was told, President Theodore Roosevelt) who came over the decades to visit generations of Coles, and to hunt and picnic on the magnificent ranch. The first president of the Republic of Kenya, Jomo Kenyatta, was a personal friend of the Coles and would sometimes showcase Kekopey, sending foreign visitors to see the rich potential of ranching in Kenya.[37]

After Independence in 1963, President Kenyatta, as a part of "Africanization," gave the Coles notice that they should sell Kekopey and be out by 1980. The Coles sold the ranch to an African agricultural cooperative in 1977, the year we left. The sale and the changes in ownership and management that followed dramatically affected everyone on Kekopey. While the idea of returning the land to African ownership is in principle the right and just thing to do, Sadiki's entire family suffered as a result. Kekopey land was divided into small *shambas* (agricultural fields or gardens) and quickly became more densely populated and agriculturally focused. Cattle herders were no longer needed. Though the Gilgil Baboon Project researchers stayed on for a few years after the sale, Sadiki never went back into the Red House. When I asked him recently just to be sure, he answered softly, "No, no, no." Gone was his privilege to cross that threshold. Sadiki's parents lost their livelihood and their home. Sadiki's parents ultimately had to return to the Samburu Reserve where poverty, unemployment, drought, and fierce tribal conflict were then and continue now to be endemic.

The changes on Kekopey also ultimately threatened the baboon population which started raiding newly planted crops and feeding in local trash pits. As a result, they were being shot and killed by the new residents. After trying to negotiate alternatives, Shirley Strum finally made the decision to translocate three of the troops to sustain the research, protect the baboon population, and see whether translocation of primates could work.[38] Strum went on to modify her own privileged research stance. On Kekopey and in the new baboon research location, she hired African field research assistants (all field workers up until then had been white outsiders) and explored community-based conservation and education projects that would benefit local communities.[39]

The colonial structures were slowly being deconstructed, bringing all the complexities of postcolonial struggles with them. During the time we lived there, postcolonial life on Kekopey was steeped in race and class myths and their strict hegemonic roles and boundaries were unquestioned. The postcolonial era had begun to blur, even confuse, some of the rigid borders and bring more ambiguity into the old established British life ways but the changes would be complicated, at times unpredictable, and very slow in coming. The aftermath of these settler colonial ideologies continues to cause pain, poverty, and violence to this day, including new and brutal tribal conflicts, political corruption, widespread poverty, poor education, and extreme privilege for the small but powerful elite Kenyan population.[40]

The second layer of colonialism that characterized life on Kekopey was more personal. While I was shocked and outraged at the British settler colonial social order, I eventually had to acknowledge that I too was a part of a privileged colonial enterprise – the western scientific enterprise that was foundational to the Gilgil Baboon Research Project. Aside from the European settlers, another significant white population in Kenya were the western research scientists. Described by Donna Haraway in detail in her book *Primate Visions*, she sees the western scientific enterprise as a constructed reality embedded in the colonial scientific discourse and in the position of privilege and entitlement of the white western scientists who conduct research, particularly primatology, in the Third World. Similar to all the other colonial extraction industries (such as mining and the export of other raw materials), foreign scientists come to these sites to take away "knowledge" for their own purposes and their own conceptions of prestigious basic research.[41]

Wa Thiong'o captures his own recognition of and disdain for this scientific colonialism in his writing about the famous paleontologist family, the Leakeys, stating that to them "it often seems that the archeological ancestors of Africans were more lovable and noble than the current ones – an apparent case of regressive evolution."[42] The African savannah was easily seen as a pristine paradise, a natural blank slate, ready for the lone white foreign scientist (often, Harraway points out, a female) to explore, exploit, and investigate. In contrast, she argues, the savannah should be understood as a scene of a much more historic and complex human–animal interaction where the researcher might be concerned about the rights of the people and their obligation to give something valuable back to Kenya.

Haraway specifically describes the Coles' colonial farm as offering a prime example of this scientific colonial utopia. She writes, "Kekopey seemed to offer the continuation of living as portrayed in the fantasy land of the film *Out of Africa*. Here was another primal scene of the Western colonial imagination, which has been as powerful for Euro-American women as men."[43] I'm not certain whether Haraway knew it when she wrote this, but Kekopey was actually the location for some of the filming of the movie *Out of Africa*.

The Kekopey baboon research would not have been possible without the colonial owners' vast land and lifestyle as well as their largesse. The two colonial systems were interwoven. The expansive acres of appropriated settler ranch lands provided the baboons with an idyllic natural home range teeming with undisturbed wildlife. There were no tourists or government agencies to deal with and the Coles provided free housing and a great deal of security and solicitous support to the researchers.

In an interview with Haraway, Shirley Strum identified Kekopey as a "baboon paradise." Strum further described her own research experience on Kekopey, stating "The Coles were extremely helpful … they thought we were crazy, but treated us like one of the family."[44] Bob Harding, the first primatologist to conduct research at Kekopey and the co-director of the project with Strum, had made the original contact and arrangements for the research with the Coles through the famed British paleoanthropologist Louis Leakey, a good friend of the Coles. The Leakey Foundation provided funding to us and many of the other primatologists who studied there over the years. The National Geographic Society provided additional support. The University of California Berkeley, the University of California San Diego, and the University of Pennsylvania, all prestigious American universities, were represented in the research mix. Richard Leakey, Louis' son and director of Kenya's National Museum at the time, was the Gilgil Project's official sponsor.

While we were in the Red House on Kekopey, we had a constant flow of distinguished international scientists visiting the site. In 1975, the kidnappings at Jane Goodall's famous Gombe fieldsite had shut their project down. Kekopey then became one of the few alternative places for scientists to observe habituated baboons up close. In addition to the primatologists, there was a network of science colleagues who were all professionally connected and would rotate through each other's research sites. In the way children that typically learn to ask "What does he or she do?" Colin would ask "What does he or she study?" A favorite game for Colin was to say "I bet nobody studies ____!" He would fill in the blank with things like "poop" or "bones" or "grass." But we had scientists pass though who studied baboon scat to examine its protein content, paleontologists studying bones, and a group of scientists from Texas A&M studying grass, measuring its growth to discover the grazing impact of wildlife on the cattle's food supply. Baboons, poop, bones, and grass. The elites of the western colonial scientific community and the elites of the Kenyan colonial settler society made up the partnership in this two-sided colonial support network that sustained the Gilgil Baboon Research Project.

Shirley Strum, in her 1987 popular book about the baboon research, *Almost Human,* describes some of the endemic colonial bigotry and tension in this "odd couple" relationship between the British aristocracy and the western baboon researchers. From the perspective of a female American primatologist, she writes:

> When I first came to Kekopey, I'd heard that most white landowners divide primates into three classes. White landowners, of course were Mark I. Natives were Mark II and baboons were Mark III. It was only in 1976 that baboons had been legally upgraded from the status of vermin to that of wildlife, and even now they were regarded as good for target practice and not much else. Female American baboon researchers were still unclassified, but I had the uncomfortable suspicion as to the category in which I fall.[45]

Aristocratic colonial landowners, privileged western scientists, and disenfranchised African laborers all shared a complicated and strictly ordered life on Kekopey. The Red House, and all who lived and worked there, sat firmly in the middle of the two overlapping colonial worlds of settler colonialism and colonial western science. They were inextricably tied together. We were all guilty. We were all complicit.

The oppressive English colonial history, our own privileged research status, and the overwhelming African poverty were potent aspects of daily life, often making Colin and Sadiki's friendship painfully controversial and presenting daily struggles for us all to clumsily negotiate. I had been a social justice educator in the era of civil rights and desegregation. I had always made certain that Colin grew up in a mixed race neighborhood and went to integrated preschools. Postcolonial life on Kekopey Ranch confronted our family with many direct and assaulting challenges to our values. Living on limited graduate student funds, our family still maintained a lifestyle that drastically contrasted with our African neighbors. We lived in the Red House. We had servants, cars, a full pantry, a kerosene refrigerator, access to medicine, education, and social networks completely unavailable to them. Although some had described the headquarters as run down, the Red House was the nicest house I had ever lived in. It had high ceilings, polished parquet wooden floors and large windows, each with its own spectacular panoramic view. Furnished minimally, it was all we could have needed and felt quite luxurious in spite of the lack of electricity or telephone. We had rudimentary plumbing, a big fireplace in the living room for the cool nights, and plenty of candles for reading at night. Other colleagues studying primates in Kenya at the time were living in tented camps and would often tease us about our elegant headquarters, calling it the "Nugu Stanley" (*nugu* means baboon in Swahili and the New Stanley is an historic luxury hotel in Nairobi).

Joab was employed as the long-time house servant by the Gilgil Baboon Research Project. When Shirley Strum overlapped with us on the hill, she added additional tented quarters and a second house servant, William. William and Joab got on well together. Both of their families lived far away in their rural home areas. Joab's wife and children occasionally came to stay on the hillside on their school holidays. But for most of the year, William and Joab were roommates and good company for each other. They did all of the daily house chores, cooking, and laundry for the researchers. They chopped wood for the wood stove where all meals were prepared and water was heated for baths. They prepared all meals from scratch, did laundry by hand and pumice stone, ironed clothes and sheets with a charcoal iron, and polished the wooden floors with sheepskin pads that they strapped onto their feet. They took great pride in their work and had relatively high status as house servants and cooks compared to many of the other ranch workers who herded cattle. It was also considered high status to work for the American researchers who generally smiled more, made eye contact, and were known to be less colonial and rigid in their social interactions. Joab was Abaluhya, and William Luo, two of Kenya's largest ethnic populations after the Kikuyu. Most of the cattle herders were pastoral peoples including Samburu, Maasai, Turkana, and Boran. There were always some tensions around the different ethnicities, language groups, and statuses on the hillside. A third group was occasionally represented on the hill. These were the Somali guards (*askari*) who were frequently hired to track down poachers and prevent any poaching of the wildlife or cattle on the ranch. The deliberate juxtaposition of tribal peoples in different, marked, and sometimes conflicting roles was also a part of the legacy of colonial Kenya and a common farm and plantation management factor in many colonial contexts around the world.

We were thrust into a world that was sheer anathema to our own long-held social justice values. I treasured being independent and recall, with a self-righteous air, telling many of the expatriates we met that we Americans took pride in doing things for ourselves. I actually met colonial adults who had never tied their own shoes, dressed themselves, or turned on their own bathwater. Even today, it is not uncommon for average families to have a domestic staff of three to five house servants.[46] It was incomprehensible to me, as much as my way of life was unimaginable (and unappealing) to them. But when we inhabited the Red House, I automatically became a *memsaab*. I hated the mere sound of the word, and the new role that went with it. The Africans used the term very respectfully as the appropriate deferential term "madam" for a white woman. But to me the word *memsaab* conjured everything deeply distasteful, if not horrifying and repugnant, about colonialism that could be read in a Doris Lessing novel.[47] I was so relieved after a few weeks, when Joab shifted from calling me *Memsaab* to calling me *Mama ya*

Colin (Mother of Colin), even introducing me to African visitors this way. It actually brought tears to my eyes the first time he used the new term of address. I hoped the choice was made because of some things I might have been doing that earned the new title and marked a new relationship. But I was almost sure that most of the motivation came from the affectionate embrace of Colin by all the hillside residents.

In spite of my new title, there continued to be a rigid social order on Kekopey and we were now a part of it. It was Joab's job to prepare food and run the house. To prevent him from doing that would only insult him and threaten his livelihood. We had to learn how to respectfully negotiate our respective roles and spaces in the Red House. There were some established rules that had existed before we came and I had to discover them as we went along. The kitchen was clearly Joab's space and there was always a slow boiling kettle of water on the wood stove ready for African visitors who might stop by to share a cup of tea with Joab and William. The kitchen opened directly to the small paved courtyard and was easily accessible without having to walk through the main part of the house.

While we had beautifully made meals three times a day plus afternoon tea and scones prepared for us and served at the large wooden dining room table, our neighbors were surviving on a diet of rationed maize meal (*posho*) and milk along with the few eggs their free-roaming chickens produced daily. I recall vivid nightmares about my guilt at not sharing our food – or even my guitar – with our new African neighbors. We had some wonderful times playing music and dancing in the courtyard on Friday afternoons. I was the only female who played an instrument – that role was reserved for African men. Women danced. In one dream, Sadiki's uncle Moses asked for my guitar so that he could "train." I said "no" and woke up crying. The guilt was constant.

In those first days and weeks, Colin too was trying to understand the extreme poverty he was seeing up close for the first time. One afternoon I saw Sadiki and his four sisters walking up the hill from our house to theirs. One sister was sliding her feet in a pair of Colin's big shoes. With one hand, another sister was hiking up a pair of Colin's shorts at her waist so they wouldn't fall down. His third sister was wearing Colin's blue and gold soccer shirt that came down to her knees. It was quite a sight. We had each brought only one suitcase with us and most of Colin's limited wardrobe was now marching over the hill. I rushed into his bedroom and asked what was going on. He looked so proud of himself as he explained it to me. Hadn't I seen that Maria had no shoes and Peninah had no shirt, and so, he said, he gave them his. I was at a loss for how to both celebrate and support his sensitivity and generosity, and to figure out how to delicately interrupt a pattern of giving that would clearly become unsustainable. But our conversation was aborted when Sadiki came back to the house and into the room holding out a basket of five eggs, sent from his mother, for Colin. I later had to explain to Colin that Sadiki's mother was obligated to reciprocate when he gave them gifts and that these eggs might have been intended for their daily family meal. His continued generosity might result in starving Sadiki's family. The economic differences were painful and glaring and it was challenging to have to explain the inequalities to Colin when I could hardly comprehend them myself. Nonetheless, "love and eggs" became a theme over the next months. Many other African ranch workers, visiting or living temporarily on the hill, would come to the house and bring "eggs for Colin" (*mayai kwa Colin*), Sadiki's good friend.

One afternoon Colin and I had gone to the little town of Gilgil nearby to pick up our mail and purchase a few items at one of the little *dukas* (shops). We saw a little boy dressed in rags and looking very sad and hungry. When we got back into the car, Colin asked what the little boy did wrong, as if his poverty could only be understood that way. I tried to explain that many of the people we saw who were so poor did everything right and that sometimes life was terribly unjust and unfair. I pointed out that Sadiki's father worked very hard herding cattle and maintaining the pumps for the ranch's water system but, as Colin could see, for all his hard work he made very little money to buy things for his children. Colin looked very serious and, lowering his head, he softly said that he would give Sadiki's father the 10 shillings he had been saving. Our life was full of these dramatic economic contrasts and we all had to figure out how to do our best to delicately and kindly negotiate our way across their marked and painful boundaries. It never felt good or right. It always was complicated. It was always a struggle.

But during the time we lived and worked there, as all of the baboon researchers before us, we were privileged western scientists, guests of Arthur and Tobina Cole on the famous and historic Kekopey Ranch. All of the Coles were kind and generous to us. Tobina was strong and straight and projected an air of both complete competence and no nonsense. Dressed in jeans and boots, she was usually covered in a thin layer of pale Kekopey dust. She managed the cattle and the dairy and seemed to know how to do every-thing. She could easily be found skillfully nursing a sick calf or shooting a trouble-making leopard that was threatening the cattle. She would give me quick and clipped advice on the spot about everything from how to nurse the orphaned baby gazelle we found to reciting directions for making may-onnaise from scratch on her way out the door. Colin was especially in awe of her. She talked to him as though he was a little adult. He seemed to rise to the occasion, responding with equal confidence. Tobina invited Colin to use the library at the main house, which he did. The library was impressive and included an extensive collection of children's books. A favorite treasure was the *Tintin* comic books she recommended highly and to which Colin and Sadiki became addicted. I would take Colin there regularly to exchange books. The Coles were always helpful, generous, and supportive. They offered us the use of their beautiful and historic house, once owned by Karen Blixen, perched on a cliff above the Indian Ocean at Kilifi on the Kenya coast 35 miles north of Mombasa where we took a memorable vacation. Berkeley Cole was always there to be supportive and we often needed his help to repair some plumbing disaster at the house or help us when we got into a fix. One night, I recall, we came back from a late dinner with friends. It was dark and as we drove up the track to the house, we found the paddock gate closed and an African man standing there and yelling loudly and incoherently at us. Colin, who had fallen asleep in the van, woke up a bit disoriented and frightened. We turned the vehicle around and drove down to the Coles where Berkeley got dressed and followed us back to the closed gate with the stranger still standing guard. Berkeley walked up to him and spoke to him kindly and quietly. Then he peacefully escorted him off in the back of his truck. It turned out he was a mental patient who had wandered off from his institution. The Coles seemed to know everything and we relied on them in many ways.

As the previous researchers had been, we were invited to formal dinners and teas at the Coles' rustic but elegant farmhouse. Shirley Strum describes her experience having tea at the Coles:

> In some ways the Coles were as foreign to me as Kekopey's wildlife or the local African culture. Visiting them at teatime was a special treat. We sat at a magnificent twelve-foot table drinking tea Tobina poured from a Georgian silver teapot, enjoying scones, breads, jams and cakes. Immaculate servants, in white uniforms with scarlet cummerbunds and fezzes attended us discreetly.[48]

"Discreet" meant that the African servants, usually two to three serving at once, were completely silent and made no eye contact. Occasionally Tobina would utter a clipped but soft-spoken side directive in Swahili telling the servers to bring or remove something, then would shift easily back to the English conversation with the seated guests. The servers were beautifully outfitted and performed their duties with grace and perfection yet all the while trying their best to be invisible as the hosts and guests indulged in favorite English foods like roast beef and Yorkshire pudding, savory dishes as final courses, and other fine delicacies the African cooks had carefully prepared in the kitchen.

On the same ranch, just a few yards away, African workers and their children ate small rations of *posho* and milk, lived in cramped quarters with no running water, plumbing or refrigeration, and suffered sometimes fatal diseases including measles, cholera, and even cases of bubonic plague. The contrasts were dramatic and painful to comprehend and to live with.

When we were invited to the Coles for supper we violated social protocol by bringing Colin with us. Young English children were usually in the care of *ayahs* and did not eat with adults. Tobina had offered to arrange for an *ayah* for Colin but I declined. English children were sent to local Kenyan boarding schools as early as four and five years old and typically off to the United Kingdom for boarding school as young as eight to twelve years old. Colin did his best to act like a little adult as we sat through long multicourse meals. But there was no possibility of bringing Sadiki with us to the Coles' table. He was a herder's son and the class and race boundaries were rigid and fixed.

Colin was convinced that when he grew up he wanted to be a "herder for Bwana Cole." I thought it was interesting that he didn't say he wanted to be a ranch owner like Bwana Cole. He and Sadiki had such fun herding the cattle in our paddock. They knew the individual names for each of the cattle. Colin had his own *rungu*, a sturdy wooden throwing club with a natural hard knotted end made from a tree root, used as a weapon and for herding the cattle. Sadiki had taught him how to use it. Colin thought it was his personal responsibility to herd the cattle away from Shirley's tent. I was sometimes quite intimidated by the large cattle, but Colin and Sadiki were bold and fearless in their work. They would come in, smiling and out of breath after their successful herding efforts, to tell me in great animated detail which cows they had moved away from Shirley's tent and how they managed to accomplish the challenging task.

In spite of the daily laughter and fun the boys had, the overt colonial racism and what Richard Conniff has referred to as the "arrogant behavior of the early British colonists"[49] that dominated Kenyan society were palpable. They penetrated every interaction. The racial tensions and dramatic economic and political inequality are well known and well documented in popular books and films like *Out of Africa* and *White Mischief*, which identified the Great Rift Valley as the infamous "Happy Valley" where white aristocratic settlers indulged in a luxurious lifestyle surrounded by African peoples in their employ who lived in desperate poverty. This racism manifested itself not only in language but in all aspects of life in the Great Rift Valley where these tensions continue to this day.[50]

Much of the social tension was manifest in everyday language use. As mentioned earlier, all interactions across tribal groups, with the researchers, and the ranch owners was in the local variety of Up-Country Swahili. English was the language of the colonizers, Swahili the more formal and distant language of government, employers, and strangers. On the hill-side, each family had its own private tribal language of intimacy in which they communicated with each other and expressed their closeness. The mere use of different languages conveyed power relationships, intimacy, and distance.

There were strong vestiges of colonialism in conveying roles and statuses when using each of these different languages, especially Up-Country Swahili which has been described as the "detested" Swahili pidgin of the colonials.[51] Consider the following excerpts from translation exercises taken from F.H. Le Breton's 1968 publication *Up-Country Swahili: Swahili Simplified,* the Swahili instruction book kept at the headquarters for the researchers. Le Breton writes that this is a book "on the sort of Swahili that all normal Europeans and Africans talk."[52] The text also painfully depicts the uneven colonial power arrangements and social order Le Breton assumes were "normal."

> Translate: Look here cook, since I ate that bread you made I have been very ill, because you cook extremely badly, also you are always late, if you do it again I shall sack you altogether.[53]

> Translate: If a woman brings a tin with much unripe coffee I shall refuse her reward. Now you, old man, your pay is ten shillings, but you have already borrowed three, there remain seven shillings. Tell the man to give out Posho, women of three tins get a whole measure, and those of only one tin do not get any.[54]

> Translate: Boy, my razor is spoilt, it will not cut even a little, I know you have used it to shave your head, and my scissors likewise, they are still dirty with your black hairs.[55]

The hierarchical social stratification is highly visible in these translation examples. Originally published in 1936, the copy at the Red House was the 16th edition published in 1968. Sadly, without any revisions, it was still widely read and used and an accurate representation of the social order in the broader society in Kenya in the mid-1970s. The extreme crude, contemptuous, and degrading stance and tone represented in these translation exercises were not directly reflected in interactions I observed with the Coles and their employees nor with the other baboon researchers and our neighbors. Nonetheless, the unequal colonial power arrangements captured in the text were still pervasive and communicated in every language choice in postcolonial Kenya in 1975.

Andrew Hill in his 1980 essay on Le Breton's text suggests that it can be viewed as a "subversive ... paraphrase book of the whole culture" and that by "selective restrictions and suggestions of [the] vocabularies" it conveyed attitudes that are "sometimes more vivid and shocking than any sociological study or historical text could demonstrate."[56] Hill observes that most of the "exercises give a flavor of the truly horrifying attitude of at least some of the elements of the colonial community." He notes that right at the beginning of the book, the verb to beat or strike, *kupiga*, is what is learned and conjugated rather than the verb to love, *amo*, which is usually learned and conjugated initially when studying Latin. Colin's father, Hugh Gilmore,[57] accurately points out what's missing in the Le Breton book. There are no exercises to translate such things as praise for excellent work, care about loved ones, shared dreams and hopes for the future, concern about children and family, etc. The Le Breton book captures much of the sickness and sadness of the linguistic hegemony of colonial Kenya and the legacy of Up-Country Swahili or Kisettla, a reduced and simplified variety of Kiswahili that was largely constructed by the British colonials themselves for their own communicative purposes with what they viewed as an inferior and subordinate indigenous African labor population. The linguist Carol Myers-Scotton describes the language situation in the following statement: "Most members of the large settler community in Kenya reinforced Swahili's image as a language for master-servant relationships with their use of a simplified version of the language consisting largely of imperatives."[58]

Myers-Scotton identifies a pattern of "ambiguity and disparity" in the history of Kenya's language policy. The Zanzibar dialect of Swahili that the British accepted as the basis for standard Swahili made its way to Up-Country Kenya not from the coast where they speak the Mombasa Kimvita dialect, but from Zanzibar through what was then Tanganyika following the caravan and slave trade routes to Kenya. Myers-Scotton claims that even though Swahili had been a recognized as a national language, many Kenyans were suspicious of it, believing it would only help them become servants and laborers for the Europeans and that English was the actual language of empowerment. Educational language policies frequently shifted over the years in response to political needs. For example, primary education was offered in Swahili from 1935. But in the 1950s, during the period of the Mau Mau Revolution, the British suspected that Swahili might become a "unifying force in developing a nationalist movement across tribal lines."[59] Primary education was then reversed to tribal vernaculars again until 1970 when English became the medium of instruction in most of the country.

Myers-Scotton captures the Kenyan love–hate relationship with English in the 1970s in several examples she provides where using English exerts power.

> I spoke English to the policeman and said I wanted to see the chief. I was allowed in. It was, I strongly believe, my English that gave me the honor to be allowed in.[60]

She also provides examples where there is resentment toward speaking English.

> At a beer party near my home, two boys broke into talk in English. The reaction from the old men was bitter ... they said ... "Are they back-biting us? Push them out."[61]

The mere use of the different available languages conveyed different relationships and historical messages.[62] For example, when Berkeley Cole, accompanied by his two huge Rhodesian Ridgeback dogs who stood tall and imposing in the back of his Range Rover, came to deliver "rations" (milk and *posho*) to the hillside workers on Fridays, he would always address the two children who would come running to greet him by saying "Jambo Sadiki" and "Hello Colin," using English to address Colin and Swahili to address Sadiki. The discursive distinction, though completely polite, marked powerful race and class messages.[63] Berkeley was being very friendly and pleasant but the mere choice of different languages to address the boys marked and highlighted the children's social and racial differences as well as their different relationships to him. Colin would exercise his prestige status, addressing Berkeley as "Berkeley" when he was with us and visiting the Coles, but in talking about him when he was with Sadiki, Colin would lower his status relationship and call him "Bwana Cole." Sadiki always called him "Bwana Cole." He did not have any other option. Colin would similarly refer to his own father as "Bwana Hugh" when speaking to Sadiki. No one ever used the term of address "Bwana" when referring to Sadiki's father, Joab or William.

Consider an example from a multilingual interaction I observed while waiting for my car to be fixed at the gas station and garage owned by our Asian friend Kirti and his family in nearby Gilgil. A large black Mercedes pulled into the gas station and a distinguished-looking African man wearing a stylish suit and sunglasses stepped out of the vehicle. As Kirti approached, the African gentleman, obviously part of the small population of African elites, addressed Kirti in Swahili, explaining that he wanted to fill the car with gas and check the fluids and tires. Kirti answered him in English, real-izing that this was an educated man who spoke English and also signaling that Kirti himself spoke fluent English as well. Now it was clear that both men spoke English. However, the African in his next conversational turn responded in Swahili again. Kirti again answered in English and the con-versation maintained that asymmetrical bilingual stance for the duration of the service encounter. The African maintained his higher status by speaking "down" to Kirti in Up-Country Swahili, the language used to give com-mands and directions to people in a service role. In Kirti's continued use of English, he was refusing to accept a lower status and asserting his higher position as a fluent English speaker.

This verbal duel was symbolic of the statuses of both languages in 1975 when English was the official language and Swahili was still struggling for recognition as a national language. In 1974 Kenyatta had declared Kiswahili a Parliamentary language, but there was drama, resistance, and controversy around that decision. Kiswahili, after decades of struggle, finally became the second official language in Kenya along with English only a few years ago, in 2010.

These colonial hegemonic language ideologies were pervasive after Inde-pendence. During the time our family lived at the Gilgil Baboon Research Project Headquarters on Kekopey Ranch, the boys' new language helped them interrupt the colonial ways of life that had been unquestioned on the ranch, in their little preschool, and in the wider social circles they regularly entered together. Kisisi seemed to symbolize new and creative possibilities amidst the growing postcolonial tensions in the shifting political landscape.

The children's language created no asymmetrical status messages the way Swahili and English did. The boys were able to resist being socialized into existing language ideologies. Instead, they created new ones. What they called "Our Language" created a free space for their friendship and a site for their discursive resistance. The two young boys acted as young social activists demonstrating their agentive ability to reshape language poli-cies and social practices through their everyday bold and fearless speech. Their everyday practices became their *de facto* language policies. They were unplanned, spontaneous, inexplicit, informal, unofficial, private, bottom up, and enacted through everyday talk. Informal as they were, they were also highly effective and transformational.

The boys' private language bonded them as much as it reflected their bonds, changing the linguistic landscape and transforming the social and symbolic order all around them. Each boy's language proficiency varied across the 15 months in the languages most readily available to them, Swahili and English. But both children demonstrated equal proficiency in one language, the pidgin they created together. Maintaining their symmetrical competence required daily negotiation, continually mediating any real and potential asymmetries in their everyday talk.

In addition to the language use that marked unequal and naturalized boundaries, there were specific territorial colonial boundaries we encountered and crossed, sometimes unexpectedly and with difficulty. No one had given me a colonial territorial map, but I could draw one now. For example, Joab and William would entertain visiting Africans in the Red House kitchen, sharing tea, debating politics and listening to the Swahili news on the radio. But only Joab and William entered the main part of the house. No other Africans crossed that threshold. I hadn't really noticed it until we had a problem. Joab was disturbed when, in the early days of the boys' friendship, Sadiki and his sisters were coming into the Red House. He would send them home. Joab was a highly respected, dignified, and hard-working man who had diligently and dutifully served the Baboon Project for more than six years at that time. It seemed that none of the previous researchers had ever violated the unspoken expectation that African children shouldn't enter the quarters. Joab and William were trying their best to sustain the appropriate etiquette – and I had not even entertained the notion that we were breaking any rules. Colin had always brought his friends "home." Laiton, Sadiki's mother, came to ask if I had told Joab to send the children home. She was crying. It took some time, delicate, and respectful negotiations, and shared tears to get all of that at least somewhat reasonably settled with Joab and with Sadiki's mother.

I am reminded of the powerfully insightful glimpses of crossing marked racialized territorial boundaries in ethnographically sensitive scenes from two films about colonial Africa. The first, *Chocolat*, is the 1988 French film directed by Claire Denis portraying life and relationships in the racist pre-Independent society in French Cameroon. The second film is *Nowhere in Africa*, the 2001 German film based on a book by Stephanie Zweig[64] and directed by Carline Link. The film describes the poignant conflict and compassion in the lives of Jewish refugees who flee Nazi Germany and come to live on a working farm in Kenya in 1938, where the colonial racial hierarchy temporarily repositions them not as pariah Jews but as privileged whites and the Africans as the stigmatized population. Both films are autobiographical about the lives of young white children, both girls, who cross into African spaces in ways their parents do not. The films visually present these borders as very marked and visceral. There is a memorable scene in *Nowhere in Africa* where young Regina, who has been told not to go beyond a certain boundary yards from their house, pauses with her feet in the red dirt at the border between her white world and the black African world. The camera focuses full screen on her feet as she makes the decision to cross into the African space. In *Chocolat*, racial boundaries between whites and native Africans are depicted as invisible but real and dangerous when crossed. Denis, the film's director, noted "In Africa nothing is ever said, but the weight of things is always there."[65] The film examines the human damage exacted on both the colonized and the colonizer.

Vivid memories of my experiences on Kekopey were evoked years later when I saw these films and recalled the "weight of things" as we tried to navigate the physical, linguistic, and psychological dimensions of the deeply divided colonial social order and the racialized spaces, territories, and boundaries that existed in order to maintain each other's othernesses.

Laiton never entered the Red House. We always talked in the court-yard outside. Sadiki's sisters stopped entering the house. I assumed it was Joab who made that decision. Neither Colin's father nor I ever entered our neighbors' houses. But both Colin and Sadiki were eventually able to move with apparent ease between the two worlds in ways we parents could not. The boys would play at each other's houses, eat each other's food, and frequently interact with both families. Sadiki's father taught them how to make arrows and he would often take them along with him when he went to the pump house. We took Sadiki with us on shopping trips to Gilgil and Nakuru, picnics at the lake, and visits to the hot springs.

It must have been difficult at first for Joab and William to serve Sadiki at our dining room table but it became a common practice and we all adapted and compromised. On Colin's sixth birthday we had a party for him. Several of his school friends were invited, as were all of the hillside children. Joab's children were visiting at the time. It was quite a wonderful event. We served food and cake for everyone outside on the outdoor patio. Afterwards I played guitar and we sang. Then we played various games. One game I had prepared for them to play was "Pin the Tail on the Baboon." I had made a large drawing of a baboon and had the detached tail for the blindfolded children to take turns trying to attach it close to the right spot. I had put the baboon drawing up on the wall inside the house in the living room and we all moved across the Red House threshold and inside to play the game. This was seven months after we had arrived and there were no raised eyebrows, no tears, and no surprises. Everyone seemed completely comfortable. Joab seemed especially proud of his two sons who were dressed up for the party wearing matching blue shirts and shorts, and having lots of fun.

In the rare cases where white children were actually allowed to play with African children, it was always unidirectional, with the white child entering the African spaces but never the reverse. For example, although most of the white colonials we met did not allow their children to play with Africans, the aristocratic Coles had allowed their children to play with the laborers' children. Tobina in a 2010 documentary[66] speaks of her own childhood, remembering going home with the cook, Meru, to his family's village three miles from Tobina's mother's home. As a little girl, she would stay with his family overnight and spend long hours there with them. But I can easily assume she never brought the cook's children into her mother's house to play.

Berkeley Cole told me that he had a friendship like Sadiki and Colin's when he was young. His friend, Seroni, was also the child of Kekopey workers and he and Berkeley grew up playing together. But Seroni did not enter the Coles' home and did not attend the same schools. Sadiki and Colin together crossed spaces and transgressed borders in both directions with their feet just as they crossed these hegemonic boundaries and spaces with their language practices.

The preschool at the Gilgil Club was the site of additional colonial exclusiveness and ultimately another of the children's colonial border crossings. Tobina had recommended the small private school for Colin when we first arrived. The school was run by an English expatriate teacher, Barbara Terry. Barbara had originally been a teacher at the historic Pembroke House Preparatory British Boarding School right across the road from the Gilgil Club. She was asked to take over the preschool when her own children were preschool age and she was available. Barbara's husband, Ray, referred to as a "Gilgil old timer" by Juliet Barnes[67] in her recent book about the Happy Valley set, worked at the nearby diatomite mine and was a bit of a local historian. The Terrys had two young daughters. They lived in one of the Gilgil Club's cottages. The Gilgil Club was a colonial leftover, a "whites only" modest country club. Apparently it is still the case that it is primarily a white space. Dana April Seidenberg recently wrote that even now "fifty years after Independence, no Kenyan of colour [has yet] become a member."[68]

In 1975 the Gilgil Country Club had lovely English gardens, a clubhouse with a library, and a few cottages. It was a place where the local colonials, mostly smaller farm owners, could gather to play snooker, polo, and golf, have drinks, attend Sunday suppers, and hold regular movie nights. When there was overflow at the Red House and the tented quarters on the hill, some of the baboon researchers from the Gilgil Project rented cottages there. Other white western researchers studying birds and other wildlife in the area also occasionally stayed at the club. Barbara and Ray always were the ones to extend themselves to the researchers to make them feel welcome and help them settle in. We all appreciated their many kindnesses. We sometimes would have competitions between the bird researchers and the baboon researchers (the birds versus the babs) playing games of snooker, an English version of billiards. This club was another space where the settler colonial and the western colonial researchers' lives overlapped and intersected.

Barbara Terry taught the dozen or so students, including her two daughters. The students all came from international wealthy homes – the children of aristocratic English lords and ladies, expatriate white Kenyan ranch managers, an African Kikuyu military general, a Dutch United Nations agricultural consultant from Indonesia, and the like. In this postcolonial period, some of the children were not white but all were from elite families. Colin started attending the preschool a few days a week. But as he and Sadiki became close and inseparable friends and as Sadiki was acquiring more and more English, we decided that Sadiki might do well to attend the same private school. This would be the beginning of a permanent commitment we would make to his ongoing education. Sadiki and his parents were very pleased and appreciative. They were anxious for the opportunities a private school education would provide for him. Sadiki's alternative community school choices were very limited and limiting.

I discussed the plan with Colin and cautioned him that some of the children at the preschool might not invite them both to play the way they had invited Colin alone. He was clear that his loyalties were with Sadiki and he would not be upset about missing some of the teas and birthday parties for the lords and ladies' children. I was proud of him. Once we had all agreed on the decision, I approached Barbara Terry. I'm sure she was more shocked than she seemed. Clearly this was an unexpected and probably unwanted request. I had to implore her to admit Sadiki as a student there. I recall her initial resistance and my tears as I pleaded my case to her. My request clearly violated the cultural expectations and boundaries in this small postcolonial community. Sadiki was the son of poor ranch workers, Nilotic peoples who herded cattle on foot for low wages and lived with all six of their children in a one-room stone dwelling with no plumbing or electricity. It was almost a local scandal when Sadiki was admitted. Barbara Terry was quite brave to agree to the arrangement. I'm sure she was wondering how the other parents would react. I had to promise that Sadiki would know his "numbers" (math skills were assumed to be lacking in Samburu children) and be washed, clean, not smell of the charcoal used by the Africans for cooking and heating, and be appropriately dressed when he arrived. Barbara was a wonderful teacher – one of the best Colin ever had – and she clearly took a risk by allowing Sadiki into the class. But Sadiki did well and she was ultimately wonderfully supportive of him. Sadiki continued his education at the Gilgil preschool for several years after we left Kenya. Barbara also helped me for many subsequent years supervise his continued schooling through secondary school, making all of the arrangements for his education at boarding schools and maintaining close contact with me as my local representative and advocate for Sadiki. To this day, Sadiki speaks of her with affection and respect.

Barbara was the only English parent to ever invite both Colin and Sadiki into her home. On several occasions, Barbara had both boys come to lunch after school and stay to play with her daughters. The Dutch and Javanese family from Indonesia did so also. Several of the English children came to visit us at the Red House where they would play with both Colin and Sadiki but Sadiki was never invited to visit them. Colin declined several birthday party invitations as a result. I wasn't always sure we did the right thing, and didn't want to hurt any of the children or their families, but it felt that it was the only thing we could do. An American ornithologist, Larry Wolf, and his wife Janet were living in one of the Club's cottages. Larry was studying sunbirds. Their young son, Allan, attended Babara's preschool also. Janet would bring Allan to the Red House to play with Colin and Sadiki. She told me later that she wanted to be sure her son experienced something other than the harsh colonial racial segregation while they were in Kenya. When Allan and the boys played together, they all spoke in English. However, the familiar Kisisi public translation rituals between Colin and Sadiki were routinely interjected in their play even though Sadiki was clearly an English speaker by that time.

The attitude toward African children was difficult and painful to comprehend. The white Kenyan settler population regularly referred to African children as *totos*. This was an Anglicized and clearly derogatory version of the Kiswahili words *mtoto* for child (singular) and *watoto* for children (plural). Using the term *toto* (singular) or *totos* (plural) served to dehumanize and distinguish African children from children in general – that is, white or European children. This pseudo-Swahili term represents a kind of covert racism similar to what linguistic anthropologist Jane Hill[69] describes in her analysis of Mock-Spanish, where phrases like "hasta banana" (for *hasta mañana*), "el cheapo", and the like might be used humorously by whites but index negative and insulting stereotypes to native Spanish speakers. When I first arrived in Kenya, I was warned, by several well-meaning English colonials, not to stop but to keep driving if I happened to hit a *toto* on the road. When I asked why, I was told I should avoid any clashes with local Africans. I didn't recognize the "Swahili" word *toto* and assumed they must be referring to an indigenous wild animal. I was shocked and appalled when I went home and looked the word up. Months later at Colin's birthday party, one of the expatriate mothers who had actually advised me not to stop on the road if

I hit a *toto* was there with her little boy. She asked if she could help me and together we actually served all of the children the birthday cake – European settler children and African laborers' children. I was wondering what she must have been thinking and was touched that she carried out the task so graciously.

Now, decades later, the word *toto* seems to have softened some of its harshest meaning and extended across racial boundaries. In recent years, Sadiki's "brother" (actually Sadiki's uncle, his mother's youngest brother) has actually signed off on his letters and emails to me with an affectionate "Your toto." But in the highly charged and racialized colonial environment in the mid-1970s, African children held complete pariah status for the colonials. Given these attitudes, it was even more striking that the boys were able to publicly declare their friendship and their equality, challenging and contesting the daunting odds against their friendship. The fact that Sadiki was actually admitted to the school, thrived, and then remained as a respected student there after we left was another example of how the two young children were able to interrupt the rigid and highly marked inequalities that surrounded them.

Sadiki's courage and confidence were striking. He knew the boundaries he was crossing. He and others clearly knew he regularly entered spaces that were off limits to poor Africans and especially to African children of the labor class. At the movie nights at the Gilgil Club, there were often a dozen or more African children outside with their faces pressed against the windows watching the movies and the *wazungu* (whites) watching the movies. Sadiki could walk proudly across that forbidden club doorway every morning with Colin. After we left to return to the States, he continued this right and privilege on his own. That must have been terribly challenging, yet he never hesitated. He and his family saw the privilege and welcomed it. And Barbara Terry stood strong as his protector in our absence.

Some of the other parents proved to be strongly supportive too. I was able to arrange for one of the other mothers, Valerie Limb, to drive Sadiki to school after we left Kenya. Valerie was the horse trainer for Lord Delamere at Soysambu. Her husband was the jockey there. Valerie had two sons who attended Barbara Terry's school. They had to drive past Kekopey on their way to and from Soysambu. Valerie agreed to pick Sadiki up if we could arrange for him to get to the main road. Every morning, Sadiki's father took him by bicycle to the main road and every afternoon he picked him up. Valerie, with her boys in tow, drove Sadiki to school and back daily. In exchange for her kind efforts, I would send Valerie boxes of azium powder, a powerful steroidal anti-inflammatory she needed for her horses that I was able to get from the Veterinary School at Penn. I was impressed and appreciative of all of their efforts, especially when we were no longer there to be direct advocates for Sadiki. Barbara wrote to me about a time when Valerie was unable to give Sadiki a lift and Barbara actually managed to get the Kenya Army to pick him up in their military vehicle! The boys' close friendship had interrupted, transformed, and opened previously fixed and closed colonial spaces and boundaries.

The boys' private language was the ultimate public symbolic badge of their friendship and functioned as a social declaration of their equality. All the way to school in the mornings, the children would chatter in the back seat in Kisisi. Once out of the car and on the school's grounds, the school rule was to speak only English. All of the children had to follow that language policy. The children who attended the little school spoke a variety of diverse languages including Dutch, French, Hindi, Kikuyu, Hungarian, Samburu, and English at home, but all spoke English at the school. I never heard about them using Kisisi at school – and children were known to tattle if the "English" rule was broken, even at recess. Colin and Sadiki, once back in the car after school, however, switched easily back to their familiar Kisisi with giggles and constant chatter.

When writing about their language in the late 1970s, I did not really focus on their language identity construction and their language ideologies. There was little if any literature in these areas at that time. Revisiting these data almost four decades later, there is a much richer repertoire of theoretical lenses and academic discourses through which to explore and express central aspects of their language practices, beliefs, and attitudes. Colin and Sadiki's pidgin language represents a compelling intersection of more recently developed multilayered dynamic theoretical influences, including studies of identity and ideology,[70] language socialization[71] and the more recently emerging field of the ethnography of language policy.[72] These concepts were present in nascent form in my original papers[73] but they were not yet a part of the articulated theoretical and descriptive discourse available to me when I was writing in the late 1970s. These theoretical concepts were pertinent as I re-examined the boys' language practices as well as the social and symbolic order they negotiated, resisted, and transformed. Language policies and practices both reflect and produce the discursive ideological positions and the social and material conditions that surround and are embedded in them.[74] Recognizing children's ideologies, Norma Gonzalez notes that "… children's fluid use of distinct language domains illustrates the dynamism of children's own language ideologies."[75]

Children are highly aware of and responsive to the social roles and statuses of different languages in their environment and regularly form judgments and make their language choices accordingly. I recall my own experience as a young child of four years riding on a public bus with my grandmother. We were both standing on the crowded bus. She held the vertical pole with one hand and my raised hand firmly with the other. As the bus jerked and swerved, I can remember trying to keep my balance by planting my feet wide apart as I held on tightly to her hand with my arm raised high above my shoulder. I wanted to get her attention but she was looking directly in front of her, out the window, and not down at me. I started to call out "Bubbie", the Yiddish word for grandmother, and the only name I had ever called her – but the word got stuck in my throat. I went silent. Somehow I knew, even as a four year old, that by calling out her name, "Bubbie", I would be announcing our Jewishness to everyone in this public space and I was pretty sure that would not be a good idea. The shame and stigma I felt in that moment embarrass me even today.

Children as young as two years of age regularly make these same kinds of language choices and demonstrate their complex awareness of and attitudes toward the social uses of the languages around them. I recall a young Alaska Native mother who was taking a language acquisition class with me at the University of Alaska Fairbanks where I taught for many years. She was anxious for her children to speak Yup'ik, her indigenous heritage language. It was a matter of deep cultural and personal pride. She came to my office in tears explaining that she spoke to her young daughter only in Yup'ik but that her child, who was just beginning to use language, would only respond in English. The child could clearly understand her mother's Yup'ik but would not speak it. Many parents struggle to maintain language vitality in heritage languages with their children. There are many such examples of young children making choices about their own language uses. A friend recently shared with me that her five-year-old Greek-American son had adamantly resisted his father's attempts to read to him from Greek children's books, strongly asserting (as if it was an official family language policy), "We don't speak Greek in this house!"

While we may not ever fully understand what young children actually consciously know about the politics and power of the languages that surround them, we see behaviorly that they are very aware of their language choices and are capable of exercising strong resistance and agency in their own language behavior. Language socialization is complex, nuanced, and negotiated, and language identity and ideology play key roles in that dynamic process.

In the case of Sadiki and Colin's language, inequities of power, race, and class are contested, resisted, and reshaped through shifting language ideologies, changing discursive practices, and sociocultural transformations that interrupt existing language hierarchies. As linguistic anthropologists Miki Makihara and Bambi Schieffelin note:

> By closely examining both the contexts of language and ideologies that give them meaning we can see how particular social and cultural formations and linguistic forms arise, continue to be effective, or come to be associated in new ways ... as a consequence of contact.[76]

These current anthropological views enrich the close re-examination of the boys' pidgin language, their creative processes of invention, and their *de facto* language policies within their cultural and ideological contexts.

Elinor Ochs summarizes the dramatic shift in the current anthropological view of children's language socialization that better captures a discussion of Colin and Sadiki's language creation. She writes:

> Children engage in multiple social worlds, become aware of social difference, and eventually are drawn into struggles for power. At the same time, they are influenced by ways of thinking, being, and (inter)acting that shift across contexts and transcend local boundaries, as traditional expectations dialogue with the effects of migration, hybridization, and globalization.[77]

Colin and Sadiki were engaged daily in multiple language and culture territorial border crossings. Sometimes they both shocked me with the fluid ease with which they traversed their complex and often intimidating linguistic and social worlds. Colin impressed me by being so unafraid of and unconcerned with the possibility of exclusion from spaces he previously had been free to access. Sadiki so impressed me when he was so strong and unafraid to enter spaces where he knew he held the pariah status of a *toto*. The fact that they managed to maintain the integrity of their friendship, their language, and their values in the face of such overt prejudice, personal threat, purposeful exclusion, and potential humiliation demonstrated their resistant agency, their risk-taking moral stance, and their loyalty to each other.

A decade after Independence, during our time on Kekopey, the colonial culture of fear and silence that Ngugi Wa Thiong'o[78] so powerfully describes was always a presence, a heavy though sometimes invisible weight bearing down. The residual fear and lack of trust from decades of brutality and betrayal on all sides were palpable. The painful memories of the brutalities surrounding the Mau Mau uprising and the Kenya Land and Freedom Army (KLFA) revolt, the detention camps and massacres, and murders – both black and white – were always just below the surface in 1975. Janet McIntosh, in her ethnographic research with white

Kenyans, describes many of the same fears, ambiguities, unsettledness and struggles of denial and belonging among the minority white population in Kenya today.[79]

The daunting "common sense" and colonial justification for such acts as Galbraith Cole's murder of a Maasai man for stealing sheep on his land still held a persistent place a half a century later. Poaching was always a concern on the ranch. Somali guards (*askari*) were regularly employed on the ranch to prevent poaching. African workers, who were extremely poor and hungry, were always looking for opportunities to get some bush meat for their families. It was not only a crime to take the landowner's domestic stock, it was a crime to take down wildlife as well. Many poachers, often workers on the ranch who daily labored hard for the owners, set up snares to catch a gazelle or other ungulates for their families. Sometimes they hunted with dogs. These were all crimes on the local ranches where the settler colonial landowners daily stood their ground. There was always a great deal of talk and tension among the ranchers around the constant threat of poachers, and strong motivation and careful strategizing on the part of local African workers to bring home extra food for their families, without risking their livelihood. The children heard these discussions often in their respective and collective social contexts. The landowners always carried guns. The African workers carried *rungus* (clubs) and *pangas* (machetes). Everyone carried a good deal of fear and mistrust.

Thomas Cholmondeley (pronounced Chumley), a classmate of the boys at the Gilgil preschool, was the great grandson of the famous Hugh Cholmondeley, the third Baron Delamere, one of the first and most influential colonial settlers in the East African Protectorate and the owner of the vast Soysambu estate. Cholmondeley was just a year older than the boys. I remember Colin proudly telling Tobina Cole that he met and knew her godson at his preschool. The Coles and Delameres were not only neighbors, but they were also related and always closely tied.

There is a bitter irony that almost a century after Galbraith Cole shot and killed a Maasai on Kekopey, and almost 40 years after we left Kenya, on April 19, 2005, the Honourable Thomas Cholmondeley, the future sixth Baron Delamere and the children's aristocratic former classmate at the Gilgil preschool, shot and killed an African Kenya Wildlife Service game ranger, Samson ole Sisina, whom he took for an armed thief on his Soysambu property. Robberies had for a very long time been rampant in the area. Cholmondeley claimed he fired in self-defense after the ranger, dressed in plain clothes, shot at him first. (Although it was reported that Samson ole Sisina was shot in the back.) The case was dropped by issuing a *nolle prosequi* (a legal term meaning "do not prosecute"). Widespread anger followed but no further action was taken against Cholmondeley. But just a little more than a year later, on May 10, 2006, Cholmondeley killed again. Robert Njoya Mbugua, a local stonemason:

> … had set out with friends to hunt for bush meat … They brought a pack of dogs for running the animals into wire snares, and they carried an iron bar for clubbing their catch and pangas, or machetes, for butchering the meat.[80]

Cholmondeley discovered them with a partly butchered impala and shot one poacher and two of the dogs. Cholmondeley claimed he was aiming for the dogs only. He did take the wounded Mbugua to the hospital, but tragically Mbugua did not survive. Cholmondeley was arrested, jailed and eventually convicted of manslaughter (rather than murder). He served close to four years in Kamiti prison, where he was the only white prisoner. The Soysambu killings and Cholmondeley's subsequent arrest, jailing and trial stirred outrage, unrest, and old resentments highlighting the strains of continued postcolonial injustices. The documentary film *Last White Man Standing* presents this case which "gripped the nation for three years," depicting Cholmondeley by some as "a racist with a trigger finger" and by others who saw the circumstances as an "embodiment of the contrast between the lives of a few wealthy Kenyan landowners and the lower castes who struggle simply to feed themselves."[81]

Janet McIntosh writes:

> Bloggers claimed that "his views on black people are still the same as his ancestors' and that he is one of many 'brutal colonists on our soil'" … Cholmondeley's case foregrounded the resentment against his family's huge Rift Valley land holdings, but also pulled to the surface the assumption that contemporary white Kenyans are susceptible to a murderous colonial arrogance.[82]

Many white Kenyans might have seen these events as a rare colonial vestige and certainly not representative of general widespread practice. I do not have any first-hand knowledge about the case and have not been to Kenya since the 1970s, but I was struck by the coincidence of knowing Cholmondeley in the context of his youth when he was a boy and a neighbor and classmate of Colin and Sadiki's. In conversations with Sadiki, I have raised questions about the case and whether he remembered going to school with him. Sadiki acknowledges that they were classmates, but has never offered any comment or opinion about the murders, arrest or incarceration.

I describe the cases of Galbraith Cole and Thomas Cholmondeley here to point to the century-long persistence of brutal and threatening racialized colonial struggles and the potential vulnerability of any African before, during, and after the period of time the children spent together in Up-Country Kenya. The fact that Sadiki, a cattle herder's son on Kekopey Ranch, was a classmate of Tom Cholmondeley in the elite white space of the private preschool at the Gilgil Club was clearly a transgression of boundaries. The children, at some level, had to be aware of the oppressive and intimidating hierarchical order and the risks they were taking just by being friends.

The ancient Greek notion of *parrhesia* means to speak freely or boldly, with the implication that there was also an obligation to speak the truth even if that would mean personal risk for those, the *parrhesiastes*, who use this fearless speech. Sharon Crowley and Deborah Hawhee[83] describe this rhetorical figure of thought as occurring when speaking out before those in power, to those who are feared, in order to exercise the right to criticize or censure some serious fault or injustice.

In modern scholarship, the French philosopher, historian, social theorist and literary critic Michel Foucault developed the concept of *parrhesia* or "fearless speech" in a series of six lectures he delivered in 1983. Foucault states:

> In parrhesia, the speaker … chooses frankness instead of persuasion, truth instead of falsehood or silence, risk of death instead of life and security, criticism instead of flattery, and moral duty instead of self-interest and moral apathy.[84]

Foucault's intention was to explore the problem of truth telling as an activity concerned with "who is able to tell the truth, about what, with what consequences, and with what relation to power."[85]

Sadiki and Colin's border-crossing loyal friendship and their invention and use of Kisisi were, in my view and by these definitions, a public act of *parrhesia*, a truth telling about equality and justice accomplished through their speech acts, their "voice without fear."[86] While the content of their talk may not have explicitly critiqued colonial ideologies and practices, their choice of a new language did. Each time they used their new language, they pronounced their strong bond, resisted the postcolonial biases, and reshaped the social structure all around them.[87] In addition to seeing the sweet embrace of their close friendship and the sheer delight they took in their daily play, I see the boys as strong young parrhesaistes exercising their unfaltering, morally driven, and purposeful actions as they fully engaged in both subtle and overt discursive postcolonial power struggles. In the face of a culture of extreme inequality, misuse of power, and a history of brutal injustice, these two young boys seemed to fearlessly use their loving, playful and bold language to disrupt the existing social order and assert their egalitarian morality.

Ngugi Wa Thiong'o[88] has described colonial Kenya as a culture of fear and silence where the repressive means for maintaining order were the sword and bullet. In the face of such intimidation, Sadiki and Colin used Kisisi to deconstruct the culture of *fear and silence* and reconstruct their own counter-culture of *courage and voice*. Their public uses of their private language are a loud and bold cultural critique. They refuse to docilely participate in the existing hegemonic colonial order and reject the language designated to keep that order in place. They resist socialization into a language ideology they reject and instead create a new language ideology that allows equal participation in their friendship.

Sadiki and Colin's defiant shared language is reminiscent of Gloria Anzaldua's description of "untamed" and "uncontrollable tongues" and their border-crossing agency.[89] The children do not confront and resist with anger or aggression. Instead, their young "wild tongues" transform with loving verbal art and playfulness. These joy-filled child language practices effectively challenge the oppressive colonial culture of fear and silence that surrounded them. Their private border tongue identified them as a distinct and separate community that valorized its own social justice values and critiqued the values of a pervasive, dominant, and dangerous settler colonial "common sense." Colin and Sadiki are two young parrhesiastes – fearless, brave, and bold speakers of Kisisi.

CHAPTER 5

KISISI: LANGUAGE FORM, DEVELOPMENT, AND CHANGE

Colin and Sadiki, and those who observed them, identified what they were speaking as a language. But what exactly did that mean? Was it a pidgin? A creole? Was it a dialect of Up-Country Swahili – a pidgin of a pidgin? A "fully-fledged" language? A jargon? Slang? A hybrid language? These questions are quite challenging to answer and are surrounded by intense and long-standing theoretical debates in the field of linguistics in general, and in pidgin and creole linguistics in particular. Allan Bell writes, "Virtually any generalization in pidgin and creole studies is controversial ... And it is a field peopled with larger-than-life characters who debate the issues with vigour."[1]

The very notion that language, as we understand it, exists is questioned by many scholars. Sinfree M. Makoni and Alistair P. Pennycook, for example, question both the idea of language and the naming of languages, claiming that "*languages, conceptions of languageness* and the *metalanguages* used to describe them are inventions."[2] To further illustrate the social, political, and ideological influences on our understandings of language and what folklorists Richard Bauman and Charles Briggs refer to as their metadiscursive regimes,[3] Makoni and Pennycook point to Judith Irvine and Susan Gal's discussion of the process of linguistic description of Senegalese languages by European linguists in the 19th century. Irvine and Gal write, "The ways these languages were identified, delimited, and mapped, the ways their

Kisisi (Our Language): The Story of Colin and Sadiki, First Edition. Perry Gilmore.
© 2016 Perry Gilmore. Published 2016 by John Wiley & Sons, Inc.

relationships were interpreted, and even the ways they were described in grammars and dictionaries were all heavily influenced by an ideology of racial and national essences."[4] Looking to find ways of rethinking language, Makoni and Pennycook argue "... we need to understand the interrelationships among metadiscursive regimes, language inventions, colonial history, language effects, alternative ways of understanding language and strategies of disinvention and reconstitution."[5]

In order to discuss Kisisi, in addition to considering the colonial ideologies of British settlers and the western research scientists discussed in the previous chapter, a third colonial lens must be considered. This third colonial lens is deeply rooted in the field of linguistics itself. Michel DeGraff [6] makes a powerful argument against what he identifies, in his controversial article, as the "Linguists' most dangerous myth: The fallacy of Creole exceptionalism." In his paper DeGraff details the ways various scholars, linguists, and nonlinguists alike, have "misapprehended the developmental and structural nature of Caribbean Creoles" and argues that "scholarly work on Creoles has for too long been tainted by certain colonial, and then neo-colonial, biases, at the theoretical, methodological, and sociological levels."[7] DeGraff describes the ways in which conceptions of Creoles and the people who spoke them were constructed by the same racist ideologies that characterized slavery, colonial subjects, and white supremacy. Makoni and Pennycook note that "DeGraff argues that creole exceptionalism was posited in order to resolve the contradiction of how, on the one hand, slaves could be regarded as speaking fully fledged languages, whilst on the other hand they were not regarded as fully fledged human beings."[8] As a result, creoles were often described as genealogically and structurally "lesser," degenerate offshoots, and structurally impoverished variants of European languages that were the norm. Studies emphasize the processes of creolization and decreolization in creole languages as if they are unique. But DeGraff points out that all languages are dynamic and undergoing change and that creoles are no different.

Makoni and Pennycook recognize DeGraff's argument that all creoles are languages but push his insight further, stating:

> Since we are skeptical of the notion of language itself, the solution is not to normalize creole languages by seeing them as similar to other languages, but to destabilize languages by seeing them as similar to creoles ... If anything we would like to argue that all languages are creoles, and that the slave and colonial history of creoles should serve as a model on which other languages are assessed. In other words it is what is seen as marginal or exceptional that should be used to frame our understandings of language. Furthermore since

most communities have been affected by colonialism and slavery at one time or another, languages without colonial history are in the exception. From such a perspective, creoles therefore should provide a prism through which we can view other languages, hence our argument that all languages are creoles rather than all creoles are languages.[9]

These arguments resonate with my own concerns as I examine and discuss Sadiki and Colin's language and the colonial linguistic ecologies that surrounded and gave rise to it. I offer the following descriptions of their language with caution. I do not present these data to support or refute any of the theoretical arguments that abound in the field. In fact, I have some concern that their story should not get swallowed up in harsh and unresolvable theoretical debates that might actually diminish the profound lessons we might learn from their meaningful personal friendship and their experiences with language invention. Instead, I present their case with the conviction that the children's surprising and unexpected language behaviors provide empirically concrete, ethnographically contextualized and close-up dynamic language-in-the-making examples that can inform many of the debates and raise provocative questions about children's multilingual and translanguaging language competencies and their role in creative language innovation in language contact situations. This is as much a story about what Sadiki and Colin do with language as it is a story about the Kisisi language itself. The children's language elevated their status, bonded them, reflected their bonds, and opened opportunities for them to cross deeply entrenched colonial borders as effective change agents and as unofficial but effective language policy makers. Most significant, it enabled their loving friendship and facilitated their daily playful interactions. Their language behaviors also convincingly demonstrate the linguistic innovations that very young children are capable of generating and performing in circumstances where there is limited shared language proficiency and cultural knowledge.

Kisisi was recognized and identified as "a language" by the boys themselves and by others who heard and observed them. I accept that local folk definition for the purposes of this inquiry. Based on my analysis of the language data, I have described their language variety as a spontaneous pidgin that shows the dynamic and continuous processes of simultaneous simplification and elaboration at work. Kisisi was a contact language that was generated by two young children who did not share a common language. It drew heavily on Swahili, the dominant superstrate language, largely following its phonological rules and syntactic structure and borrowing heavily from its lexicon. In its earliest phase of the language genesis, it reflected the simplification (pidginization) of forms typical of pidgin languages, including a restricted lexicon, unmarking, absence of copula (the verb *to be*), articles and inflection, preverbal negation, polysemy (many meanings for a word), and circumlocution (many words for fewer ones and figures of speech). Yet, with the expansion of the function of the language to express more fully all of the communicative needs two close friends have beyond limited play contact, the data indicate there was expansion and developing complexity of the language form as well. There are many examples of simultaneous and continuous lexical and syntactic elaborations (creolization), including a constantly building lexicon incorporating loan words, compounds and numerous neologisms, the introduction and reappearance of articles and markers, and the development of novel tense and aspect markers. All of these features indicated nascent forms of creolization. This is particularly striking since the language "lived" for such a short period of time, only 15 months, and had only two speakers. Upon hearing the children speak Kisisi, two things were clear – their language sounded like Swahili, but was unintelligible to a Swahili speaker. The following discussion presents lexical and syntactic examples from the data and includes several transcripts of the children's verbal interactions, demonstrating the uses of their language in a range of discursive contexts and actual "here and now" vignettes of their dynamic language-in-the-making creative and playful processes of invention and metalinguistic negotiations.

Kisisi Lexicon

Colin and Sadiki's language had five lexical classes, enumerated below. Briefly, there were loan words from Swahili and from English, modified words from Swahili and from English (including morphophonemic and/or syllable reductions and calquing), and many newly invented words, neologisms, that drew heavily on sound play, onomatopoeia, repetition, and reduplication.

Swahili Words

As in most pidgins, many of the things indigenous to the environment (i.e., wildlife, food, places, plants, and specific local objects, tools, and weapons) were frequently named in Swahili. For example, a traditional wooden club (*rungu*) and the colorful patterned cloth traditionally worn by women (*kanga*) were unique to the context and no equivalent English words were known to Colin. All of the species of wildlife in the area were among the first Swahili words that Colin learned. The English equivalents were the first to be forgotten. A few months after we arrived, Colin asked, "How do you say *duma* (cheetah) in English?" William Samarin[10] notes this type of memory loss and obsolescence is common to pidgin situations. Food names also were exclusively borrowed from Swahili (e.g., *bread/mkate, tea/chai, water/maji*). Most of the loan words from Swahili were used to represent exactly the same meaning in Kisisi as they did in Swahili. Greetings, farewells, and politeness terms (e.g., *hello/jambo, goodbye/kwa heri, thank you/asante*) were some of the first Swahili words Colin learned and were also central in Kisisi interactions.

Although much of the lexicon was taken from Swahili directly, it is interesting that a number of the Swahili words that were known and used by both children with considerable regularity when speaking to others, never appeared in the taped dialogues between the children when speaking Kisisi. For example, the children routinely and early on used the Swahili word for fast, *pesi pesi*. They used the word when speaking to Africans and understood it, responding appropriately when they were directed to do things *pesi pesi*. Yet they never used the word with each other in the recorded data. Instead, they invented their own numerous alternative neologisms for expressing speed, going fast, and driving fast. These included the lexical items *diding, tena*, and *gningininge* mentioned in Chapter 3. *Diding* is sometimes alternated with *ddnn*, which often was translated by Colin to mean *driving*. It also appeared that the sound *neoow* was in the process of becoming lexicalized to mean *fast* also. They commonly used the Swahili words *namna hii/like this, viatu/shoe, tayari/ready* when speaking to Africans. But when speaking to each other in their private language, these same lexical items were expressed in their own language *tena/fast, las/like this, boot/shoe*, and *redi/ready*. (See the section below on neologisms, or newly invented words, for further discussion.)

Modified Swahili Words

Various modifications of Swahili words occurred in Kisisi. While their pronunciation largely followed the standard Up-Country Swahili pronunciation, there were certain variations. Below is the "pronunciation guide"[11] taken from the Le Breton Up-Country Swahili language instruction publication discussed in Chapter 4. While not linguistically informed or sophisticated, it is the description that was used and accepted by speakers.

Certain phonetic variations from the Swahili pronunciation Le Breton outlines above were used regularly by the boys. For example, velar stops shifted from voiceless to voiced as in Afri<u>c</u>a > Afri<u>g</u>a. These phonetic patterns were consistent when modifying English words as well. Phonemes were sometimes added to words. The Swahili *naenda* (present tense marker *na-* + *go*) becomes *nawenda*, adding the *w*. Quite common and often inconsistently used are a variety of morphophonemic reductions. The following examples are illustrative of this type of truncation.

English	Up–Country Swahili	Kisisi
I, me	mimi	mimi or mi
you	wewe	wewe or we
trip	safari	safari or fari
car	motakaa	motaga or ga
finished	kwisha	sha

Another type of modification of Swahili was calquing or compounding. Several examples were presented earlier (see Chapter 3) and included lexical phrases such as *kubwa moto / big fire* for the sun and *maji choo,* meaning urinate, literally *water feces.* Another example of compounding was offered by Colin when we told him the Swahili word for train was *traini.* "Oh, we call it *motoga moto* (car fire)," he responded. These types of lexical inventiveness commonly found in pidgins are full of metaphor and imagery and provide an indication of the elaborative process at work.

English Words

Many English words appeared in Kisisi with no modifications, for example, *stop, outside, run.* Often used were "comic book" words like *pow* (crash) and *bang* (bang). I also included in this category *huh* (what) and *uhuh* (yes) and the corresponding negation, *umum* (no). However, English verbs were generally preceded by the Swahili present tense marker *na-* (e.g., *nastop, narun*). Similarly, in Sheng, the form of modern urban Kenyan youth language discussed in Chapter 2, the Kiswahili infinitive prefix *ku-* is used with English words as in *kuded* (to die).

Modified English Words

Morphophonemic reductions were not restricted to Swahili words. Even when speaking English, Colin would often say *tend* rather than *pretend.* *Tend* was a frequently used word in Kisisi as well. Most modifications of loan words from English followed the phonological rules of Swahili. Yet there were several unique Kisisi variations that were used regularly and systematically and are detailed below.

Voicing changes

Dental fricative	θ → ð	*voiceless → voiced*	thing → ðing (as in "them")
Velar stop	k → g	*voiceless → voiced*	take it → tegid
Alveolar stop	t → d	*voiceless → voiced*	jacket → jegid

Place of articulation and manner of articulation change, with optional voicing change

v → p or b	*labio-dental fricative → bilabial stop, voiced or voiceless*	slave → slep (or sleb)

In Kisisi *take it* becomes *tegid*. *Okay* becomes *oge* or *ge*. *Slave* becomes *slep* or *sleb*. Occasionally the modification adds syllables, as in *cowboy* to *kalaboy*. Oppositely, reductions in syllables, such as the following, occur.

English	Swahili	Kisisi
like this	namna hii	lathas or las

In the early phase of Kisisi the children often said *lathas* but later it was frequently shortened to *las*. This is very similar to reports in children's use of *Tok Pisin* by Gillian Sankoff and Suzanne Laberge,[12] where adults will say *Mi go long haus*, a child will often say *Mi go laus* for "I am going home."

Newly Invented Words

Many of the new words in Kisisi grew out of sounds that were made during play, particularly car sounds made while the children played with toy match box cars. As mentioned earlier, *tena*, *diding*, and *gninginge* all meant to go fast, and all sound like the noises made when playing with their racing cars. *Ddnn* was also used alternately with *diding*. As mentioned above, it also appeared that the sound *neoow* was in the process of becoming lexicalized to mean *fast* also. *Pesi pesi*, the Swahili word meaning *fast*, was quite well known to the children yet they created numerous new lexical items to replace it in Kisisi. There was a very high use of these neologisms in their play interactions. This heavy relexification of words in specific areas is discussed by Halliday as a feature of anti-languages, jargons, and cants of subcultures that "set it off most sharply from the established society."[13] The areas of relexification are focused on the subculture's central activities where there might be an extensive lexicon, for example for tools of the trade for criminals, which might include types of criminal acts, kinds of criminals and victims, etc. For law enforcement, the lexicon might be expanded in areas of penalties, prisons and the like. In these examples, Halliday suggests that these lexical features make it "seem somewhat larger than life. The language is not merely relexicalized in these areas: it is *over*lexicalized."[14] This appears to be the case for Kisisi where Sadiki and Colin actually overlexicalize in the areas of speeding car play, scatological toilet activities, and "naughty" humor.

Another type of lexical creativity in Kisisi involved reduplication commonly found in pidgins. *Kiki* was the Kisisi word for *break* or *broken*. Although I was not able to identify a specific etymology, it appears to have had its origins in a crashing sound something like an explosive sound as in "*kissshh*." The boys made this play sound when they made cars or trucks crash into each other. (The English word *crash* is actually considered to have an onomatopoeic origin.) The sound effect *kissshh* was then probably modified phonologically to *ki* and then reduplicated to *kiki*. This processual modifying pattern is quite similar to the examples described earlier for *diding/fast*. *Kiki* was often reduced to *ki*, but the truncated version did not apparently affect its meaning. Additionally, it was sometimes used with *nawenda* (go) for example, *Road nawenda kiki*, meaning *The road is broken/broke*. In the same way, *nawenda* was used with *ded* (die/dead), e.g., *nawenda ded* (go dead/die), which as noted above is similar to the Sheng use of the infinitive *kuded* (to die). Sometimes the boys use *kwenda ded* or *kuenda ded,* both meaning *going dead* or *dying.*

There are co-occurrences, alternations, contrasts, and redundancies in the development of the lexicon, many of which seem to have no significant cause. In Swahili, the word for *come* is *kuja. Kuja* was used in numerous ways in Kisisi as well. Yet the English word *come* was used in Kisisi also. However, the English *come* or *cumin* was only used after a noun phrase and with *is* or *'s* as in *moja pupu's cumin (a fart is coming).*

Other redundancies are interchangeable such as the three words mentioned above, *diding, tena,* and *gninginge,* all meaning *fast* or *go fast* (depending on the word order of the sentence). Similarly, there are a number of ways to say *no* in Kisisi, drawing on both English and Swahili. *Uhuh, no, hapana, hakuna,* or *si* + verb all mean *no*. All were used interchangeably in any situation.

Kisisi Syntax

Just as there are cases where many words can mean the same thing (polysemy), there are several interesting cases of one word meaning different things. This will lead into the topic of syntax, because when such words vary in meaning, the variance is usually dependent on word order placement and the appearance of serial verbs or verb strings (e.g., such as in English, *will have gone*).

Fixed word order is one of the common characteristics of a pidgin. The coding and encoding responsibilities of the speaker/hearer are somewhat reduced in this way, since the pidgin usually has little or no inflection (e.g., suffixes, prefixes). The word order of Kisisi reflects this feature. Up-Country Swahili, similarly, is not highly inflected and relies on word order for clarity. There is much influence of the pidginized Up-Country Swahili the children knew in Kisisi. DeCamp has noted the stimulus diffusion that takes place when speakers familiar with any form of pidgin create a new pidgin.

The language that results from such a situation will be influenced by the previously known patterns.[15] This is no doubt true in the case of Kisisi as well. However, it is interesting to note the original patterns that emerge within such a setting, for in the variation one can see linguistic flexibility and creativity in operation.

Unlike Swahili, Kisisi followed the English rule for the position of adjectives.

English	Up-Country Swahili	Kisisi
many cars	motakaa mingi	mingi motaga
	(car many)	(many car)

The modifier always precedes the noun in Kisisi. It always follows the noun in Up-Country Swahili.

Another English characteristic of Kisisi is the occasional use of the 's placed after a noun to represent the verb *is* where there would have been none. Note the following example.

English	Up-Country Swahili	Kisisi
The car is coming.	Motaka nakuja.	Moja motaga's cumin.
	(Car coming.)	(One car is coming.)

Where this 's appears, the feature of copula absence begins to be modified. Though the close details of the ontogeny of the language are not fully documented in these data, it appears that elaborations such as the appearance of this 's and the two examples that follow were incorporated into Kisisi in the later stages of its use and development.

The Changing Uses of *Moja* (One)

The following example of syntactic inventiveness presents the Swahili word for *one/moja*. The children used this word to represent number, just as the Swahili usage indicates. For example, they would count *moja* (one), *mbili* (two), *tatu* (three), in Swahili. Or if asked how many they wanted of something, they might answer *moja*. But, as described in the section above on lexicon, some Swahili words in Kisisi took on expanded functions and meanings. *Moja* was a word like that. It was used very frequently and in a variety of ways.

In the following language sample, an analysis of the word *moja* and its various changing and expanding uses and the playful manipulation of sound, function, and meaning will be illustrated. The word was used in a variety of contexts and took on a number of functions according to the context in which it was used. The uses of *moja* in the examples below occurred while the children were taking turns swinging on a rope swing that Colin's father had hung from a tree in the yard. As described earlier, the boys would run, grab the hanging knotted rope, swing for two to three times, counting off each swing, and then jump back to the ground. In this context, *moja* was used over and over in a chanted counting sequence: *moja/one, mbili/two, tatu/three.* When they landed, they sometimes called out *sha sha/finished* (*sha* is a truncated and reduplicated form of *kwisha*). The children counted off their swings as they took turns hanging on to the flying rope. They filled their ongoing repetitive physical game with continuous and repetitive verbal play as well as giggles. This was especially favored as an activity in the early weeks, along with their soccer games. They would play for hours. Sometimes Sadiki's sisters would join them and they would line up to take turns. Their usage of *moja* in the following examples is completely consistent with the Swahili usage.

During this rope swinging episode there was considerable verbal play with the counting sequence routine. A few examples of this play routine follow.

(The boys are taking turns swinging on a rope swing and counting off *one, two, three* in Swahili as they each swing up to three times.)

EXAMPLE 1

Sadiki:	Tatu. Wapi wewe?
	three where you
	(Three. Where are you?)
Sadiki and Colin:	Moja, mbili, tatu.
	(One, two, three.)
Colin:	Silly tatu. Wapi wewe?
	silly three where you
	(Silly three. Where are you?)

EXAMPLE 2

Colin:	Moja.
	(One.)
Sadiki:	Uhuh moja.
	(Not one.)

Colin: Ndiyo moja.
       (Yes, one.)
Sadiki: Moja, mbili, tatu. (laughing)
       (One, two, three.)

EXAMPLE 3

Colin: Redi au uhuh?
       (Ready or not?)
Sadiki: Redi, moja.
       (Ready, one.)
Colin: Nne.
       (Four.)
Sadiki: Mbili. (laughing)
       (Two.)

The play with numbers in the counting sequences illustrated here provided an opportunity to use the word *moja* over and over again. The repetitive structure allowed for playful variations within the routine framework. The children could make big jokes with minor unpredictable manipulations of the basic routine. The boys were running, jumping, swinging, and verbally joking all at once. All the while, they were simply counting from one to three. In example 1, as they swing, Sadiki calls out *wapi wewe?* (where are you?) as he flies high in the air. Next they sing out the numbers in chorus together as Colin swings. Then Colin substitutes the rhyming *silly* for *mbili* (two) and repeats Sadiki's phrase *wapi wewe?* (where are you?). There is a poetic rhythm and repetition as well as a physical rhythm and repetition to their counting play. In example 2, they play with *ndiyo/yes* and *uhuh/no,* interrupting the predictable counting pattern and laughing at their own defiant teasing alternations. In example 3, Colin asks Sadiki if he's *ready or not (redi au uhuh),* and Sadiki answers that he's ready and starts to swing, calling out *moja/one.* Colin teases substituting the number *nne* (four) for *mbili* (two), which makes Sadiki laugh. Each of the boys knew these Swahili counting words well. They listened when the uniformed army troops marched nearby on the dirt road near the hillside doing their maneuvers and rhythmically counting off *moja, mbili, tatu.* The boys often imitated them, pretending to be soldiers by marching and counting in Swahili, too. It may have been through this type of repetitive use and manipulation that *moja* originally started to expand its function and use.

As time went on, I was struck by the frequency with which they used the word *moja* throughout their discursive interactions. In everyday uses of Swahili, the word *moja* would be heard only rarely, either in counting, *moja* (one), *mbili* (two), *tatu* (three), or in answer to a question such as, *How many? Moja.* When listening to the children speaking their language, however, the increasing frequency and use of *moja* were striking and noticeable. Both children used it repeatedly and in a variety of sentential environments. The repetitious rhythm punctuated every utterance with multiple tokens of its use. I could see that they clearly were not simply using the word for counting.

The following dialogue will illustrate the frequent and expanded uses the children made of *moja* in Kisisi beyond its original Swahili meaning.

The children are playing with rocks, pretending the rocks are cars. They are narrating their familiar "Slave Safari" game (discussed in Chapter 3), pretending that Batman (Sadiki) and Action Man (Colin) are saving slaves from being captured by robbers (slave traders). All of these actions take place in a modern-day setting of the African Safari Rally. Sadiki has asked Colin for one of the cars. Colin refuses, saying the one Sadiki has is the same. Note the repeated uses of *moja* and the steady appearance of it in most utterances. I have emboldened *moja* to highlight its uses.

Colin: Uhuh. Na **moja** sem lathas.
         (No. That one is the same as this.)

Sadiki: Thas uhuh. Thas uhuh.
         (This isn't. This isn't.)

Colin: Uhuh. [car noises] Thas ga na **moja** tena motaga.
         (No. [car noises] That car is a fast car.)

Sadiki: Mimi nataka xx. Na mi nawenda. Ah, hakuna **moja**.
         (I want xx. So I can go. Ah, this isn't one.)
         Moja thas kwa kuwenda. Mi mawe's hakuna kabisa. Ah thas sem.
         (One of these for going. My rock is gone completely. Ah, this is the same.)
         [Sadiki finds one that pleases him, and they continue to play.]
         Moja thas slep. **Moja** thas sema. "Wewe diding nyumbani?"
         (This is a slave. This one says, "Are you going fast to your house?")
         "Jua **moja** road?"
         ("Do you know the road?")

Colin: Wewe diding **moja** nyumbani? Wapi nafanya **moja** road?
         (You're going to the house? Where will you make the road?)

Sadiki: No enda.
(I can't go.)

Colin: Oge. Fanya **moja** road, kwish thas road nawenda kiki. Ge?
(Okay. Make a road, this road is finished it has broken. Okay?)

Sadiki: Ya. Mimi nafanya.
(Yes. I will make one.)
[The boys begin to build a road on the floor.]

Listening to the sound of the repetitions of *moja* in the above transcript, one cannot avoid the conclusion that there is a special rhythm, meter, and sound that are being played with, in addition to the semantic and syntactic play.

The following examples of *moja* examine the use a little more closely. It seems that *moja* can represent an article (*the* or *a*) preceding a noun, as in the following examples:

(1) **moja** road
(a road)

(2) **moja** nyumbani
(the house)
(**moja** + noun)

Moja apparently can also have pronoun status either used alone or with *thas/this*. Consider the following:

(1) Ah, hakuna **moja**.
ah no **one**
(Ah, that's not one.)

(2) **Moja** thas kwa kuwenda.
one this for to go
(One of these for going.)

Moja was also frequently used with *na*. *Na* is a special case in itself and will be discussed below. *Na-* can be a present tense marker accompanying all verbs in Kisisi (and in that usage, it is shown with a hyphen to indicate that it is incomplete without a verb). For example, even when English verbs are used, *na-* will precede them as in *nastop* or *narun*. *Na* also means *and*, in Kisisi and in Swahili. The following example illustrates several uses of the *na moja* occurrence.

(1) Thas ga **na moja** tena motaga.
this car **na one** fast car
(This car is a fast car.)

(2) Nataka **na moja** chai?
na want **na one** tea
(Do you want some tea?)

(3) Wewe diding au **na moja** ga?
you go fast or **na one** car
(Will you go fast or will the car?)

It seems that, as with the co-occurrence with *thas*, the general effect is to emphasize the determiner (e.g., article, pronoun) quality of the word. Yet there seem to be some verb overtones in its use with *na*. For example, is there an absence of copula (i.e., the verb *to be*) in example 1 above, or is the *na moja* an attempt to fill the void of a verb? Consider these sentences, taken from a different play session.

(1) Mimi **moja** pow.
me **one** crash
(I went crash.)

(2) **Moja** diding.
one fast
(He goes fast.)

The use of *moja* with verbs (*moja* + verb, *na* + *moja*) suggests that it might be in the process of change in the direction of some auxiliary function.

All of these examples demonstrate that *moja* has considerably elaborated its meaning and its syntactic function far beyond its original use in Swahili. *Moja* is clearly being manipulated and experimented with by both children. A detailed analysis of the uses of *moja* indicated that it was gaining determiner status, representing an article, and also having pronoun status. This seems strikingly similar to the extended use in *Tok Pisin* of the word *wanpela* (one fellow), which has similar determiner functions. The data also indicate that *moja* appeared to be expanding its functions to serve as an auxiliary with certain verbs.

Another example of syntactic elaboration in Kisisi is the use of *na*. In Swahili, *na* can mean *and*, *also*, *by*, or *with*. In Kisisi, only *and* and *also* are represented by *na*. The other most common meaning of *na-* in Swahili is as a present tense marker. *Li-* is used for past tense and *ta-* for future in standard Kiswahili (note: *li* and *ta* are infixes— never prefixes, like *na-* can be in the first person — but for simplicity's sake, they are not represented with a hyphen before and after the infix). The local Up-Country Swahili overuses the present tense *na-*, and *li-* and *ta-* are seldom used. In Kisisi *li-* and *ta-* even more rarely appear, and the present tense marker *na-* is most frequently used with verbs. Below are two examples of *na* as commonly used in Kisisi.

(1) Wewe nataka wenda swing?   na + verb
you want go swing?
(Do you want to swing?)

(2) Wewe majinga na mimi silly   na = and
you fool and me silly
(You are a fool and I am silly.)

There are several occurences of *na* in the data that indicate the use of *na* in quite a different way. Consider the following examples.

(1) Mimi ju na mimi boot nawenda kiki sasa.
me know na me boot went broke now
(I know that my boot is falling off now.)

(2) We jua na mingi polisman na sema.
you know na many policeman na say
(You know that many policemen talked.)

The first example was said by Colin in early April, the second by Sadiki in late May. These occurences indicate that *na*, a word that is redundant and obligatory in Kisisi utterances to begin with, shows the possibility of becoming a marker for clausal embeddings in sentences. In both cases, the use of *na* follows the verb *to know*. In both cases, it is followed by a noun phrase plus a verb phrase. A marker in such a position can help to clarify the message for the listener.

Tense and Aspect

The final examples of grammatical change and elaboration in Kisisi focus on tense and aspect. These examples illustrate some of the devices, semantic and grammatical, that the children used to communicate temporal and aspectual relationships in their speech. (An important consideration to keep in mind is that the boys' language was created based on their competencies as young children and not adults, but it is beyond the scope of this discussion to explore these developmental distinctions in any depth.) To more closely examine the range of possible ways in which the children expressed tense and aspect, I examined frequently occurring verb strings (e.g., *will have gone*) for possible auxiliaries and original tense markers. The following examples describe some of the innovative devices, semantic and grammatical, Sadiki and Colin used for expressing temporal relationships. The analysis will also illustrate instances where their communication was not efficient given the lack of a shared means of expressing certain dimensions of time.

Research on the topic of tense and aspect explores how different languages treat these dimensions of verbal expression. Pidginization and creolization processes in languages offer an excellent data source for the investigation of how patterns of systematically expressing tense and aspect originate. Pidgins are usually described as lacking markers of tense and aspect, whereas creoles not only possess but share many characteristic ways of treating these temporal relations.[16] As a result, a logical question arises: how do tense and aspect begin to appear in a creole, and what semantic and grammatical forms do they take?

A brief mention of the way in which tense and aspect are defined will be helpful at this point. Dan Slobin[17] explains the term tense as the temporal contour or placement of events in relation to their speech acts. Comrie offers the following definition:

> [A]lthough both aspect and tense are concerned with time, they are concerned with time in a very different ways … [T]ense is a deictic category, i.e., locates situations in time, usually with reference to the present moment, though also with reference to other situations. Aspect is not concerned with relating the time of the situation to any other time point, but rather with the internal temporal constituency of the one situation; one could state the difference as one between situation-external time (tense).[18]

In the discussion that follows, an attempt will be made to illustrate the ways in which the children expressed tense and aspect, providing a profile of the various dimensions described in the above definitions.

The common verb forms that appear in Kisisi most frequently are the unmarked verb and the present *na-* + verb. Most commonly, the unmarked form appears to be used as a simple past or as a command. The *na-* marker is used to the almost complete exclusion of the other possible tense markers used in the Up-Country Swahili spoken in the area, i.e., *ta-*, the future marker, or *li-*, the past tense marker. Though *li-* and *ta-* were sometimes used in the broader speech community, the children used these markers only rarely. *Ta-* appears in the entire corpus only three times and *li-* only once. Each of these cases will be discussed in more detail in a later section. The high frequency of the use of *na-* with verbs in Kisisi confirms reports of the excessive use of *na* in Swahili pidgin and in what Wald[19] has referred to as "Down Talk" or "Foreigner Talk" in Mombasa Swahili.[20] This is also the most common form of tense used in Sheng, a form of urban Kenyan youth language, as noted in the discussion in Chapter 2.[21]

To more closely examine the other possible ways in which the children may have expressed tense and aspect, frequently occurring verb strings were examined for possible auxiliaries and/or original tense markers. In the following examples, some innovative devices for expressing temporal relations and contours in Kisisi will be demonstrated.

Expressing Nonpunctual Temporal Aspect in Kisisi

Nonpunctuality or "durativity simply refers to the fact that the given situation lasts for a certain period of time."[22] A punctual situation, on the other hand, is "one that does not last in time" but takes place "momentarily."[23] In spite of the fact that the local Up-Country Swahili had no formal means of expressing durativity, it appears from the data that the children created forms for this type of aspectual distinction in Kisisi.

Enda

The first example of durativity in Kisisi is the use of the Swahili verb *enda,* which means *go.* The word appears with several variations, with no change in meaning, in Kisisi, including *enda, kuenda, kuwenda, kwenda, wenda, nawenda,* and *naenda.* In addition to its having various pronunciations, it functions in a variety of ways.

The common Swahili use of *enda* is illustrated in the following Kisisi examples.

    (1)   Naenda wapi?
           na go where
           (Where are you going?)

    (2)   Mimi na enda Gilgil.
           me na go Gilgil
           (I am going to Gilgil.)

(3) Mi na enda room kwa is mimi's kwisha.
    me na go room for is me's finish)
    (I am going to my room because I'm done.)

In each of the cases above, *enda* is used to indicate directionality. As in the Up-Country Swahili the boys knew, these Kisisi sentences all use *enda* to depict the action of going someplace (e.g., to the town of Gilgil, to my room).

Benji Wald[24] identifies *enda* as an auxiliary in Mombasa Swahili. From the few examples he offers, it still appears to be used for directionality, even as an auxiliary. Consider this example from Wald (note that Wald capitalizes the tense markers LI and TA):

niLIkuwa niTAkwenda kusoma Uhuru Garden
"I was gonna go read in Uhuru Garden"[25]

Although the future form of *enda* (*nitakwenda*) precedes the infinitive (*kusoma*) *to read*, it seems more to be clarifying the fact that the person is going *to* Uhuru Garden in order to read, rather than expressing some relationship between *going* and *reading*.

Both the examples 1 through 3 above and the reports by Wald show *enda* in its conventional directional usage. The remaining examples from Kisisi appear to be original uses the children created to express temporality. The next examples show the use in Kisisi of *enda* as an auxiliary with states.

(4) Colin: Enda mimi boot nawenda kiki sasa na kuja.
           go me boot go break now and come
           (My boot keeps falling off over and over.)
           Hakuna mbaya.
           no bad
           (It's not bad.)

    Sadiki: We na boot nawenda ki.
           you na boot go break
           (Your boot keeps breaking/falling off.)

(5) Colin: Mimi ju na mimi boot naenda kiki sasa.
           me know that me boot go break now
           (I know that my boot is flying off now.)

(6) Sadiki: We naenda dead?
           you go dead
           (Are you dying?)

Examples 4 through 6 show *enda* followed by *kiki* or *ki* (break) and *dead*. Used as an auxiliary with these words, idioms are created.

nawenda kiki/goes break/broken – is breaking
naenda dead/goes dead – is dying

Possibly, these idioms indicate that the act of breaking or dying took some duration of time, that they did not happen punctually but happened slowly – even sometimes in slow motion – and dramatically. The data are inconclusive in this regard, but there is enough of a suggestion to consider the possibility.

Colin's utterance in example 4 contains several elements that suggest duration of time. (This example was also described earlier in Chapter 3.) During the utterances in 4 and 5 above, Colin was swinging on a rope swing while wearing loose rubber Wellington boots, or Wellies. Each time he would swing out on the rope swing, his boots would fly off and fall to the ground. The "game" was repeated over and over, and the boots fell off each time. It was amusing and fun. He says, *Hakuna mbaya* (It's not bad). Certainly in this context the aspectual notion of iterativity, or repeated action, was evident. It had become part of the fun to have the large boot slip off while he was flying though the air on the swing. Both children were delighted. Notice that *enda* is used twice in the sentence: at the very beginning and then again with *kiki*. There will be more discussion below about the use of verb repetition as a way of depicting duration of action. For now, let it be noted that the repetition of *enda* may express the fact that the boots fall off again and again.

Another interesting phrase in example 4 is *sasa na kuja* (also mentioned earlier in Chapter 3). Roughly translated, this might mean "now and coming." *Sasa* is the adverb *now*. *Kuja* is the verb *to come*. It is easy to see that the phrase might suggest that the continuous action of the boot episode is happening now and will happen again in the future. *Kuja* seems to indicate future time in this context. There will be a more detailed discussion of *kuja* below in which its role in suggesting future time will be elaborated.

The above examples show the use of *enda* with states. The next set of examples illustrate the use of *enda* with action verbs.

(7) Colin: Mingi slep nawenda diding.
 many slave go fast
 (Many slaves are going fast.)

(8) Sadiki: Nawenda pow
               go crash
               (They are crashing.)

(9) Sadiki: Naenda kuja lathas motogas.
               go come like this cars
               (These cars will be coming.)

(10) Sadiki: Mimi wenda tegid motoga. Neyow!! [sound effect]
               me go take car neyow
               (I am taking the car. Neyow!)

In each of these examples *enda* is in a preverbal position in the sentence, and the verb that follows it is always unmarked (i.e., does not use the *na*-tense marker). The function of *enda* in this context seems to be that of an aspectual auxiliary or marker of durativity. Much of their pretend play was described as it was being enacted. As the utterances were spoken, the children were pushing match box cars, rocks, and small action figures across the floor, playing out cooperative vignettes. It was important to know what each player was doing so that the next actions would fit the scene. Their play dialogue in these interactions was mapped on to the actions. In many of these instances the actions were ongoing and continuous. One can see why it would be useful in such contexts to distinguish punctual and nonpunctual actions. The next set of examples will illustrate this point further.

(11) Sadiki: Wenda sema lathas "Nevwee".
               go say like this nevwee
               (You say this, "Nevwee".)

(12) Colin: Nawenda stop lathas
               go stop like this
               (Stopping like this.)

(13) Sadiki: Thas motoga nawenda like this.
               this car go like this
               (This car is going like this.)

In each of the examples 11 through 13, *enda* is used in similar fashion to examples 7 through 10. The addition in these last three examples, however, is the use of *lathas* or *like this* following the main verb (*enda* + verb + *lathas*). The use of the expression *like this* always accompanies a continuous demonstration or an extended acting out with play props of some sort and therefore necessitates the nonpunctual aspect.

One further example of durativity with *enda* is its occasional use in the following way: *naenda standing* (go standing), or *naenda jambing* (go jumping). In these cases, the English progressive ending *ing* seems to serve the same function as did *lathas*; that is, it reinforces the continuous nature of the activity.

Repetition and Reduplication

Other devices in Kisisi for expressing nonpunctuality are the uses of repetition and reduplication, which are also quite characteristic of pidgins and creoles. The following examples will demonstrate this strategy.

(14) Sadiki: Kula moja tire mingi kubwa kula moja tire.*
eat one tire many big eat one tire
(I am eating many big tires.)
[*the tire refers to bread baked in the shape of a tire]

(15) Colin: Ddnn ddnn wewe leg?
drive drive you leg
(Are you driving your leg fast?)

Sadiki: Ddnn ddnn mi leg.
drive drive me leg
(I am driving my leg fast.)

(16) Sadiki: Tend two thousand mingi policeman kuja sasa sasa.
pretend two thousand many policeman come now now
(Pretend two thousand policemen come right away.)

In example 14, Sadiki and Colin are having tea together. (A longer excerpt was discussed in detail earlier in Chapter 3). They are eating the breads they have baked in the shapes of tires, tractors, and the like. The freshly baked breads are piled on a plate in the center of the table. The repetition of the phrase *Kula moja tire* suggests beautifully that the eating of these many breads will be a continuous nonpunctual activity.

In example 15, the children are pretending to drive their legs! This action requires steering over the knee and hopping about. The main verb *ddnn* is a rasping sound play vocalization modified by spelling in these examples. Often the word for *drive* (*diding*), also meaning *fast*, was produced with more careful phonological adaptation to Kisisi pronunciation, but even in its more playful sound effects form, its meaning is apparently the same. The strategy here for indicating the continuous aspect of the action is to reduplicate the verb, even in its sound play form.

A final example is offered in 16, where *sasa* (now) is reduplicated to indicate that the policemen are coming right away. In Up-Country Swahili the expression for *immediately* is *mara moja*. They knew and used that term often with others but they used *sasa sasa/now now* with each other in Kisisi. *Mara moja* does not appear at all in the recordings of the children speaking Kisisi. Apparently, *sasa sasa* conveys the same meaning. In example 16, Sadiki uses the word *tend*, which means *pretend* in Kisisi. This is an interesting case and will lead us into the next section on irrealis or unreal time.

Expressing Irrealis in Kisisi

Irrealis, or unreal time, includes future, conditional, subjunctive, and the like. In Kisisi, the children were able to express irrrealis in a variety of ways.

Tend

In Kisisi, statements that begin with the word *tend* (a reduction of *pretend*) clearly signal unreal time. Several examples follow.

(17) Colin: Tend wapi wenda kiki road. "Road nawenda kiki."
pretend where go break road road go break
(Pretend where we go, the road breaks. "The road is broken.")

(18) Colin: Tend mingi nawenda uko boat, oge?
pretend many go there boat okay
(Pretend many people go there to the boat, okay?)

(19) Colin: Tend nawenda pow hakuna nakwenda dead.
pretend go pow not go dead
(Pretend I crash but I don't die.)

Sometimes the *tend* statements are descriptive of actions that will be enacted following the utterance. In other cases, the statement sets the stage for other actions and is not demonstrated but provides the background information required to make sense of the activities being played out. Consider the examples above. In example 17, Colin says, "Pretend where we go, the road breaks." This irrealis statement sets the scene for the next sentence, delivered in an actor's voice within the play scene: "The road is broken." Irrealis statements like the one in this example are usually marked by a shift in tone and register that marks the statement further as "outside" the play scene and are directed to the other speaker, who should receive it not as an actor in the play scene, but as his outside persona. Examples 18 and 19 function as manipulators of the flow of play activity. Each statement begins with the command to *tend* (pretend) and marks a decision about how the play should follow it.

Kucheza

In Kisisi, the Swahili counterpart to the English loan word *tend* is the Swahili word *kucheza* (to play) or *cheza* (play). It appears to have the same meaning as *tend* and also functions to signal pretend play and unreal time. The examples that follow will illustrate some of its uses.

(20) Colin: Cheza fari wenda uko.
play safari go there
(Play that the safari goes there.)

(21) Sadiki: Enda kucheza thas ... naenda sema kwa tegid mimi Afriga.
go play this go say for take me Africa
(Play like this... go ask to take me to Africa.)

(22) Colin: Ogay. Kwa kucheza moja kwa shooting kwa hapa
okay for play one for shooting for here
(Okay. Play that this one is shooting here.)
Kwa shooting mimi, kwa shooting mimi machine gun.
for shooting me, for shooting me machine gun
(He keeps on shooting me with a machine gun.)

(23) Sadiki: Na wewe kucheza mimi ndiya. Sema "Ju ki."
and you play me yes. say know break
(And you play with me, okay. Say, "I know it broke.")

(24) Colin: Kwa kucheza wewe nini?
for play you what
(For play who will you be?)

(25) Colin: Kucheza hakuna ju nawenda.
play no know go
(Play you don't know where to go.)

(26) Sadiki: Ona kucheza thas. Kucheza kwa motoga slep
look play this play for car slave
(Look, you play this. Play the car with the slave.)
nawenda ddnn nawenda ddnn motoga.

go drive go drive car
(Keep driving very fast.)

(27) Colin: Ndiyo kucheza mi ddnn thas. Thas slep dead.
              yes play me drive this this slave dead
              (Yes, play I am driving this fast. This slave is dead.)
              Ingine slep is cumin. Na shooting kwa motoga ingine
              another slave is coming shooting for car again
              (Another slave is coming. I am shooting from the car again.)

A very frequent utterance in Kisisi, *Kwa kucheza wewe nini*? (For play, who
will you be?), appears in example 24. This was a frequent routine-like question that often opened play sequences as well as terminated other activities.
What follows *kucheza* in many other cases is a rehearsal for the play scene.
Instructions and lines to recite are offered, as in examples 21, 23, 25, and
26. In example 27, *kucheza*, in the first sentence, marks the entire narrative
as unreal time.

Derek Bickerton[26] has suggested that all markers for tense and aspect
can combine in creoles and that they will do so in an invariant order: ante-
rior, irrealis, and nonpunctual. He further adds that the meaning of irrealis,
when combined with nonpunctuality, is "a non-punctual action occurring
in unreal time,"[27] that is, a future progressive. The examples above offer
several such combinations with irrealis where the nonpunctual aspect is
marked by *enda* (e.g., examples 21 and 26) and/or repetition (e.g., examples 22, *kwa shooting,* and 26, *nawenda ddnn*).

Although there is good reason to believe that examples such as 22 and
26 use repetition as a means of expressing duration, one caution must be
noted. As mentioned earlier, children's language differs qualitatively from
the language of adults. It is possible that these repetitions are sometimes
false starts typical of child language. Nonetheless, the data build in a way that
provides convincing evidence that the children were performing significant
grammatical elaborations of Kisisi in order to express tense and aspect.

Kuja

Kuja is the Swahili verb *to come*. In Kisisi, *kuja* appears to function in much
the same way that *go* does in Anglo-Creoles[28]; that is, it appears to function as an irrealis marker to denote future tense. Consider the following
examples.

(28) Colin: Tend we ask for the one. "Get in. Kuja hapa Afrigan.
              tend we ask for the one get in come here African

(Pretend we ask for this one. "Get in. Come here African.
Hapa jail.
here jail
(Here's the jail.) [makes verbal click sound as he locks cell]
Kwisha naenda Afriga."
finish go Africa
(You're finished going home to Africa.")

(29) Colin: Kuja nawenda dead is go hakuna ingine.
come go dead is go nothing again
(When you die, nothing more happens again.)

(30) Sadiki: Naenda kuja lathas motogas.
go come like this cars
(Cars will be coming like this.)

(31) Colin: Kwa saa sita kuja.
for six hours (noon) come
(When noon comes.)

(32) Colin: Kuja kwisha nataka wewe nataka nini?
come finish want you want what
(When you're done, what do you really want to do?)

(33) Colin: Kuja mi na kuchez the swing Sadiki... sha... sha
come me play the swing Sadiki... done... done
(I'm going to play on the swing, Sadiki... finished...
finished.)
Sasa mimi na sema kabisa. Now I'm gonna play
now me say enough now I'm gonna play
(Now I said enough. Now I'm gonna play.)
the swing, okay? [to tape recorder in English]
(on the swing, okay?)

(34) Colin: Mimi ta kuja mkati kesho asubuhi.
me ta come bread tomorrow morning
(I will have my bread tomorrow morning.)

(35) Colin: .... ready, mi ta kuja.
... ready, me ta come
(... ready, I will come.)

(36) Sadiki: Nataka shooting. Slep ta kuja.
want shooting slave ta come
(I need to be shooting. The slave will come.)

In example 28, Colin first speaks in English, then code switches to Kisisi when he says "*Kuja hapa Afrigan*" ("Come here African"). This first use of *kuja* is typical of both Kisisi and the original Swahili usage; that is, it is used in an unmarked form and functions as a command to come. The brief narrative in this example is mapped on to the familiar play scene in which the children are pretending that they are "bad guys" capturing escaped slaves and sending them back to America. In the last sentence of the narrative sequence, the use of *kuja* seems to have a rather different function. It seems here to act as an irrealis marker for future time. Consider the sentence just before the last one in example 28: "*Kwisha na enda Afriga.*" Colin tells the prisoner that he's finished going to Africa. *Kwisha* (finish) is a Swahili verb that can denote completed action. It is also used as an auxiliary with infinitives to form a perfect tense in Mombasa and Standard Swahili (see Wald, 1973, for further discussion of this use; also Polomé, 1972). Heine (1973, as cited by Wald) has observed additionally that in Nairobi Swahili, *kwisha* has replaced the past tense marker *li-*. In Sheng, *kwisha* functions similarly but has been reduced to *sha*; *sha* also appears in Kisisi, even though the boys had never heard that reduction. These reports are helpful in analyzing the use of *kwisha* in Kisisi. What can be noted in the present example from the Kisisi data is that the two sentences are marked initially as strong contrasts in past and future time, the first sentence beginning with *kwisha/finish* (past) and the second beginning with *kuju/come* (future). This is reminiscent of the contrast in time mentioned earlier in this discussion in example 4, when *sasa/now* and *kuja/come* were contrasted to depict the iterative aspect of Colin's boots falling off.

In several examples above (e.g., 29, 32), *kuja* is used where *kama/when* might have been more typically used in Up-Country Swahili. For instance, example 29 is glossed "*When you die nothing more happens again.*" The gloss for example 32 is "*When you're done what do you really want to do?*" Each implies unreal time in the future. Example 31 uses *kuja* with the lexical time marker, noon, further indicating its reference to future time. In example 33, Colin and Sadiki are playing together outside with the cassette tape recorder. Colin addresses the tape recorder in Kisisi first, then gives a brief translation in English. His own English gloss, *gonna*, indicates future time, which further suggests that *kuja* in the first sentence denotes future time.

The final three examples in this set are most interesting in light of this argument. In each case (examples 34 through 36), *kuja* is preceded by the Swahili future tense marker *ta-*. These three cases are not common; in fact, the tense marker *ta-* appears rarely in the Kisisi data. Example 34 therefore includes the future tense marker (*ta-*) plus a verb that conveys irrealis aspect (*kuja*) and two time adverbials (*kesho/tomorrow* and *asubuhi/morning*) in order to ensure, with numerous devices, the communication of future time.

As in the case of expressing duration of activity, it appears to be important in Kisisi dialogue to express future temporal distinctions. Planning play before enacting it is crucial to the interactions and is therefore needed in the communicative repertoire. As a result, there are multiple innovations that the children have generated to meet the needs of their speech situation. The innovative uses of *tend, kucheza,* and *kuja* all mark these temporal meanings and pragmatically facilitate the imaginative play activity so central to their interactions.

Taka

One final set of examples warrants discussion. The Swahili verb *taka/want* is frequently used in Kisisi. It is also commonly used in Up-Country Swahili. It is used conventionally to ask whether the interlocutor wants something, e.g., "*Nataka na moja chai?*" ("Do you want some tea?"). In Kisisi, it is often used to ask whether the interlocutor wants to engage in some activity, as in example 37 below.

(37) Colin: Wewe nataka wenda swing?
              you want go swing
              (Do you want to swing?)

(38) Sadiki: Nataka las swing, oge?
               want like this swing okay
               (Do you want to swing like this, okay?)

(39) Sadiki: Wewe nataka wenda moja?
               you want go one
               (Do you want to do one?)

(40) Colin: Wewe nataka wewe mingi raining?
              you want you many raining
              (Do you want lots of rain?)

(41) Sadiki: Wewe nataka do thas.
               you want do this
               (Do you want to do this?)

(42) Colin: Nataka naenda room then lete moja jegid swi na go outside.
              want go room then bring one jacket so we go outside
              (I want to go to my room then bring a jacket so we can go
              outside.)

The frequency of *taka* in the data suggests that the children are repeatedly checking out with each other whether or not they are in agreement. Along with *taka*, *oge* (okay) is an often repeated expletive, which seems to further ensure mutual participation and agreement in the children's interactions. Because the communicative channel is a very delicately constructed one for these two speakers, they are regularly checking out its effectiveness. It also appears from the data that the children engaged in dialogue that was not heavily marked with lengthy narratives. It may be that if the narrative went too long without checking out the interlocutor's understanding of it, the speaker ran a much higher risk of being misunderstood. (It also should be noted that as an adult/parent outsider, I might not have been able to observe and record more lengthy narration that was possibly going on in private when the boys were alone.)

In addition to its function of checking out the other speaker's desires, *taka* appears to be used as an inceptive. Aston[29] has described *taka* in this way, suggesting that it means to "be on the point of" doing something.[30] Wald's analysis of Mombasa Swahili indicates that *taka* shows a tendency to assume the characteristics of a future tense marker, much in the way *kuja* functions in Kisisi. The notion that *taka* might function as an inceptive in Kisisi is best illustrated in example 42 above, when Colin explains that he is about to go to his room to get his jacket so that they can go outside.

The examination of how notions of temporality were expressed in Kisisi demonstrates that those areas of time which were most frequently used in the children's speech situations, i.e., contextual and (pretend) play, were the areas of most demanding need and therefore the primary focus of their efforts at linguistic elaboration. The need for and development and use of devices, features, and formulas for expressing future tense and irrealis mood – which were absent in Up-Country Swahili – were a pragmatic need for the children, who regularly planned narrative play sequences in advance and had a need to distinguish clearly that they were planning for play scenes that had not happened yet but that would be enacted in the near future. As they played out and narrated their imaginative scenarios and vignettes, they also needed to express subtle and dramatic differences in grammatical aspect differentiating between ongoing continuous actions, repetitive and habitual actions, punctual and durative actions, and the like. These were key distinctions for conveying more nuanced meaning in their dramatic imaginary narrative play performances and benefited from their rich and creative grammatical innovations.

The boys were continuously maintaining Kisisi through their daily shared discursive practices, which served to constantly revitalize and grammatically develop their shared in-group private language. The striking symmetry in their verbal performances was notable and achieved through constant interaction, including their discursive devices, such as repetition, to achieve symmetrical performance, and through metalinguistically checking each other out regularly to be sure they were comprehending meaning. The areas of strongest linguistic elaboration reflected their imaginary play activities and focused on their speech community's values, identity, and ideologies.

Miscommunication, Maintenance, and Repair

In all of the previous examples, the children display the symmetrical nature of their competence in the language and their shared lexical and grammatical understandings. But this was not always the case. There were also times when they miscommunicated and when their translanguaging proficiencies differed. The following two close-up interactional examples will illustrate their discursive negotiations in these more challenging communicative situations.

Example 1: Expressing Past

In the following interaction, the children are unsuccessful in communicating the temporal aspects of their interaction. The analysis of how they struggle to negotiate and renegotiate meaning will be informative. The interaction takes place outside the house, near a tree with their rope swing. The children are alone and, at my request, the tape recorder is on. Sadiki is trying to ask Colin if he would like to listen to what they have said on the tape recorder so far. Colin does not understand Sadiki's request and misinterprets what he is saying. Sadiki's use of *li-*, the Swahili past tense marker, in line 8 of the transcript below is a rare occurrence in the data. Sadiki's reliance on his own more advanced competence in Swahili (i.e., using *li-* to denote past) appears useless with Colin, who apparently still does not understand that Sadiki is not referring to what Colin has *just* said (simple past) but to what they *had* been saying for the last 15 minutes on the tape.

> (1) Sadiki: Wewe nataka sema sasa/si jua ... oh ... eh... thas.
> you want say now we don't know oh eh this
> (You want to know what we said now/we don't know...
> oh... eh...this.)

(2) Colin: Kwa kucheza, ogay so mimi nataka enda na swing ogay…
sha sha.
for play okay so I want to go and swing okay done done
(For play, okay so I want to go swing, okay…done, done.)

(3)   Kuja mi na kucheza the swing, Sadiki… sha sha.
come me play the swing Sadiki done done
(I will play on the swing, Sadiki… all done.)

(4)   Sasa mimi na sema kabisa.
now I say enough
(Now I said enough.)
[They take turns on the swing and talk briefly.]

(5) Colin: Mimi najua moja run moja tree na swing. Wewe najua?
I know one run one tree and swing you know
(I know how to run to the tree and swing. Do you know?)

(6) Sadiki: Narun na moja tree kwa uko swing – wewe nataka jua
nasema?
run na one tree for there swing you want know say
(I know you run to the tree and swing there – [now] do
you want
to know what we said?)

(7) Colin: Nini?
what
(What?)

(8) Sadiki: Wewe nataka jua si lisema, is wap… sema sijui?
you want know not li say is where say not know
(Do you want to know what we said before… we don't
know what we said?)

(9) Colin: Uh uh mimi nataka jua swing hakuna ingine?
no me want know swing nothing again
(Do I need to explain to you about the swing again?)

(10)   Gay sasa ona/swing sema moja las/so nataka tegid ona las…
running kwisha.
okay now look/swing say one like this so want take look
like this … running finish
(Okay now look/I'll explain how you swing like this/so
you need to take it like this, look, and finish running.)

(11)   swing mrefu... jua sasa? U huh like Afrigan swing
            swing far know now yes like African swing
            (Swing far... do you know now? It's like an African swing.)

(12)   uko Afriga nawenda na jua las kwa uko.
            there Africa go know like this for there
            (You know you go like this over there in Africa.)

(13) Sadiki: Mimi najua latha swing. Wewe na ona! [annoyed tone]
            I know like that swing you look
            (I know how to swing like that. You watch me!)
            [Sadiki swings.]

(14) Colin: Um hum.

(15) Sadiki: (inaudible) xxx

(16) Colin: Uh uh... riding mi horse kwa Pembrook... sha.
            no riding my horse at Pembrook ... finished
            (No... riding my horse at Pembrook... all done.)
            [TAPE OFF] [TAPE ON]

(17) Colin: Ogay. Sasa mimi hakuna jua nini mi sema so bas
            okay now me no know what me say so enough
            (Okay. Now I don't know what I said so we'll stop.)

(18)   Know what I said? I said I want to stop a bit

(19)   because we want to listen to what we hear. So just stop a
            bit ogay.
            Be back soon.

In line 1, Sadiki asks Colin if he wants to know what they said now (on the tape recorder). However, Colin understands it to be a request for him to say something now. In lines 3 and 4, Colin says that now he has talked enough for the tape recorder and he and Sadiki are about to play on the swing. In line 6, Sadiki again tries to ask Colin if he is curious about what they have said on the tape: *Wewe nataka jua nasema?* (Do you want to know what we said?). But again there is nothing in the utterance or in the immediate context to let the Colin understand that the statement refers to something that occurred in the past. Colin confirms this with his question in line 7, *Nini?* (What?). At this point, Sadiki attempts to clarify the confusion about time by using the Swahili marker *li-* to establish past tense. Colin still does not understand and thinks that Sadiki is saying that he doesn't know what Colin has said about how to swing (line 5). Colin therefore goes into a lengthy demonstration of how to swing, slowly describing his actions as he performs and then twice (lines 11–12) asking Sadiki if he now understands. Sadiki's frustration with Colin's didactic behavior, in addition to his lack of understanding, can be heard in Sadiki's annoyed tone when he delivers line 13, declaring that he quite well knows how to swing that way. Sadiki then tells Colin to watch him as he further proves his own swinging competence. Colin acknowledges this as he looks on at Sadiki's swinging demonstration saying, "Um hum." Line 15 is a statement by Sadiki that is inaudible – possibly he is suggesting at this time that they turn off the tape recorder, so as not to further document their linguistic failures. But Colin, who still does not understand, begins telling Sadiki about the time he saw this type of swing at the Pembroke School when he went horseback riding there. In the middle of his utterance the tape recorder is shut off, probably by Sadiki. It will never be known just how the children repaired their communication, but it is clear that in some way, while the recorder was off, Sadiki communicated with complete accuracy to Colin. When the tape is once again on, Colin finally demonstrates that he knows what Sadiki wanted to do and now shares the same goal. He too now wants to listen to what they have been saying on the tape. When Colin tells the tape recorder in pidgin what he is going to do, he uses no past markers. Even when he explains to the tape recorder in English he does not say that they want to listen to what they *said* but to "What we hear." This suggests his own developmental limitations for expressing past tense. Yet they have managed to understand each other and now share the same meaning for these words. The process with which they managed this will remain a mystery, but the ultimate success of their communication is documented and will remain an inspiring testimony about the human ability to communicate in spite of apparent linguistic limitations and obstacles.

This example shows that the children did not have elaborated linguistic devices for placing events in past time. The facility with which the children express themselves about present and future stands in striking contrast to the hard work that went into communicating about the past. We can assume that they did not frequently use their language to discuss temporal complexities of past experience but instead that their language functioned mainly to facilitate contextual activity and future planning. I do not mean to suggest that the children never discussed their pasts with one another. Though clearly their creolizing efforts are most apparent in present and future temporal and aspectual distinctions, that is not to say they could not communicate about past time. The example above provides evidence that in spite of their limited linguistic resource, they were still able to get the past temporal message across.

Although their pidgin was largely symmetrical, it was constantly developing and changing, causing continuous need for discursive work involving interactional repetition, repair, negotiation, adaptation, innovation, and creative meaning making. Almost all of this maintenance work was embedded in play and play-related activities.

Example 2: *Kila Siku*

The next example demonstrates the range of the boys' different language limits and proficiencies and how they negotiated them, especially, as in this case, when there were misunderstandings. This interaction shows the boys collaboratively traversing the overlapping language domains and complex linguistic ecologies of their social world. The example highlights Sadiki's multilingual proficiency and communicative competence. It was clear that Sadiki was fluent in Samburu, that he had more proficiency in Swahili than Colin, and that he could code switch easily from English to Swahili and Samburu as well as to Kisisi.

The transcript highlights their different language proficiencies and the translanguaging practices they used in an everyday speech event. They demonstrate their communicative competence, appropriately using different languages for different audiences and different purposes.

This interaction was recorded 10 months after we arrived, on a voice letter that Colin was going to send to his grandmother. I was in the room recording the two of them. They were each six years old by the time of the recording. Colin and Sadiki speak to each other primarily in their language. Some English is used when Colin is addressing his grandmother on the tape. Colin asks Sadiki to say some things in Samburu for his grandmother, who is the ultimate audience for their verbal performance. As Sadiki responds to these requests to speak in Samburu, Colin attempts to negotiate the translations and mediate the discourse. However, Sadiki's Swahili proficiency makes this a challenging task for Colin. Sadiki, at one point in the discourse, uses the Swahili expression *kila siku,* which means *every day.* Colin clearly does not know or recognize the Swahili expression. Sadiki and he have to work out their miscommunication using their shared language, Kisisi.

(1) Colin: Sadiki ni nini ngombe kwa Kisamburu? [in Kisisi]
                      Sadiki what cow in Samburu
                      (Sadiki, what is "cow" in Samburu?)

(2) Sadiki: Ngishu. [in Samburu]
                      (Cow.)

(3) Colin: He just told you "cow" in Samburu. [English to grandmother]
[I make some other suggestions about what he might say, and then Colin turns the tape recorder off and privately, softly, and inaudibly speaks to Sadiki in Kisisi, possibly explaining more about his grandmother; he then turns the tape recorder back on and they continue.]

(4) Colin: (inaudible) xxx sema kwa Kisamburu.
(xxx talk in Samburu.)

(5) Sadiki: Sema ninyi?
(Say what?)

(6) Colin: Mingi.
(Lots.)

(7) Sadiki: Oge. [Samburu utterance – xxxxxxxxx.]

(8) Colin: Nini wewe nasema?
What you say
(What did you say?)

(9) Sadiki: Uh (pause) mm, mm.

(10) Colin: Nini wewe nasema, Sadiki?
What you say Sadiki
(What did you say, Sadiki?)

(11) Sadiki: xxx piga mpira kila siku na Colin. [in Swahili]
(xxx kick the ball every day with Colin.)

(12) Colin: Nini wewe nasema, Sadiki?
What you say Sadiki
(What did you say, Sadiki?)

(13) Sadiki: (laughs)

(14) Colin: Nini wewe nasema, Sadiki?
What you say Sadiki
(What did you say, Sadiki?)

(15) Sadiki: Mi nawenda kwa mingi na leo piga mpira kwa mingi. [in Kisisi]
I am going for many today kick the ball for many
(I am kicking the ball every day.)

(16) Colin:	He said that every time we kick [In English to his grandmother]
(17) Colin/Sadiki:	the ball [both boys speak simultaneously in English]
(18) Colin:	every d—d um day! [silly, playful voice]

In this brief interaction, Sadiki demonstrates his competence in the range of language varieties available to him. He also displays his ability to participate with appropriate language choices in a single speech event to multiple overlapping audiences for a variety of purposes. In line 7, Sadiki produces an utterance in Samburu, as Colin had requested. In line 8, Colin asks him, in Kisisi, what he said, expecting him to translate the Samburu. Sadiki hesitates in line 9, saying, *Uh…mm, mm.* Sadiki is possibly considering just how to translate the Samburu. In line 10, Colin asks again, repeating in Kisisi, *Wewe sema nini, Sadiki?* (What did you say, Sadiki?). In line 11, Sadiki responds with a Swahili translation in which he uses the phrase *kila siku*, Swahili for *every day*. In his performance for the tape recorder, I assume he chose to respond in Swahili rather than Kisisi to be more formal and polite in this public performance for an elder, Colin's grandmother. He knew the recording was going to travel all the way across the ocean to the United States. Possibly in line 9, Sadiki had not only been considering how to translate the Samburu utterance but also deciding which language might be most appropriate for this specific occasion. The Swahili would certainly be considered more formal and appropriate for an elder he didn't know. But Colin clearly did not understand the Swahili expression *kila siku* and asks Sadiki again, in line 12, what he said, *Nini wewe nasema?* (What did you say?). Recognizing that Colin does not understand him, Sadiki laughs but still does not answer his question in line 13. This buys Sadiki a little extra time to sort out how to proceed. In line 14, Colin, still in the dark, again asks what Sadiki said: *Nini wewe nasema?* (What did you say?). In line 15, Sadiki finally code switches to Kisisi, saying, *Mi nawenda kwa mingi na leo piga mpira kwa mingi* (I am kicking the ball every day), or as Colin translates it in lines 16 through 18, *every time we kick the ball every day.* It is clear that after repeatedly asking Sadiki what he had been saying, Colin finally and immediately understands his friend and the complex Kisisi utterance in line 15. This code switch provides a perfect example of a direct translation from Up-Country Swahili to Kisisi and illustrates some of the children's original, sophisticated, and newly invented elaborated grammatical structures.

This recording was made 10 months after we arrived, and the children's language had by then developed some sophisticated and elaborated ways to express time and temporality, or tense and aspect. These elaborations were much more complicated than the local Up-Country Swahili and more typical of the more complex syntax forms developed in the creolization process in pidgins all over the world. The linguistic elaborations were also much more complex than the initial simplified pidgin the boys initially created to communicate 10 months earlier. Their private language was dynamic and had been continually expanding lexically and syntactically. Kisisi, at this point in time, had developed several linguistic devices to show the ongoing, repetitive, iterative, and habitual character captured in the adverbial phrase *kila siku* (every day). The use of the phrase *kwa mingi* (for many) is repeated twice in line 15, both before and after the verb phrase. This common repetition pattern in Kisisi is used for emphasis and to mark continuous action over time. The same utterance also uses an additional syntactic innovation to further represent the daily ongoing aspect of their morning soccer ritual and ball-kicking play. *Nawenda* is a Kisisi variation of the Swahili present tense marker (na-) with the verb *to go* (enda). *Nawenda* is used here as a serial verb, functioning as an aspectual marker to show the ongoing action of the present tense (*na-*) of the verb *piga* (kick). The present tense marker is used along with the noun *leo* (today) to further emphasize that the time of the kicking action is not only now, in the present, but even more specifically, it is this very day. Kisisi therefore employs numerous complex lexical and grammaticalized devices to show the habitual aspect of the action of their daily soccer play, instead of using the simple phrase *kila siku* (every day). Colin's quick comprehension of Sadiki's response is immediate and striking as he translates the utterance into English for his grandmother ("He said that every time we kick the ball every day" in lines 16 through 18). He did not know the phrase for *every day* (*kila siku*) in Swahili, yet he translates the complex Kisisi utterance using the exact English phrase *every day*. It is interesting to note that he repeats *every* twice in his translation (lines 16 and 18). Possibly, he is using repetition as a device for added aspect in his English version. Sadiki also demonstrates his comprehension of all of the shifting language terrain, chiming in with Colin in English as they both say *the ball* simultaneously in line 17. Sadiki is clearly following, even anticipating, all of Colin's English translations.

These examples of the boys' discursive negotiations in the two speech situations detailed above show their creative verbal competencies, linguistic flexibility, and unrelenting determination to persist, negotiate, and work out verbal conversational strategies for meaning making even in challenging communicative interactions where limited shared proficiencies compromise understanding.

While the language data are compelling and these examples provide significant insight into how the two boys negotiated meaning with their limited invented language repertoire, I will never know how they were able to communicate about the full range of their shared experiences, thoughts, and worldviews in their private verbal interactions. For example, consider their behavior when they turned the tape recorder off so that they could negotiate privately to resolve their miscommunications about expressing the past in example 1 above. There were many private times when they discussed things that I was not able, or allowed, to observe or record. Knowing their somewhat limited vocabulary, I would sometimes wonder at what they could possibly have said to each other in Kisisi to produce some of the insights Colin shared with us that seemed to reflect their having had conversations about deep cultural and philosophical knowledge. For example, one afternoon while we were eating lunch, Colin began to explain to his father and me that Africans don't believe in one god but in many. He said there were many spirits and these were in everything. When we asked him more about these ideas, he started pointing to the things on the table saying that it was like this: "There's a god of sandwiches and cheese and mayonnaise ..." He went on and on. Possibly Sadiki had been explaining these ideas to him while they sat in the bush where Sadiki could have similarly pointed to nearby objects like plants and rocks and animals. I don't know how he learned about these religious concepts, but clearly they had managed to discuss abstract beliefs that went conceptually far beyond enacting character pretend play roles in races and robberies with good guys and bad guys. On another occasion, Colin offered, "That's not Joab's real name." When I asked him to explain what he could possibly be talking about, he offered that for Africans it is considered disrespectful to call someone by name and since white people always do that, the name Joab was offered to the ranch employers to avoid being insulted. I called "Joab" *mzee* (elder) or *mwalimu* (teacher) after that. I still wonder how these abstract and complicated concepts of appropriate cultural practices, such as naming, terms of address, and the uses of honorifics, could have been discussed in Kisisi by Sadiki and Colin. But clearly, they had discussed and understood them.

It has been said that all languages can express the concepts that are needed by their speakers. But if that happens not to be the case, people will find a way to make their language fit their needs.[31] These speculations were proven true on a small hillside in Kenya where two young children made their language express their needs as children, as playmates, and as close friends. Their complex and ongoing verbal interactions provide a rare glimpse into children's striking abilities to create completely novel and fresh language innovations that were never heard or spoken before. These innovations reflect patterns of creative linguistic variations and innovation used in multilingual contexts all over the globe and throughout history. Kisisi provides a "truly remarkable real-life pidgin birth"[32] that can inform debates on pidgin and creole creation. The case of the children's private language adds a vivid and dynamic linguistic example that can contribute to our understanding of the nature of language and the processes of invention that underlie its origins and genesis.

Sadiki and Colin drew on their linguistic competencies, sophisticated grammatical strategies, and lexical invention techniques that helped them overcome limited means of communication when they did not share the same language proficiencies. Their linguistic mechanisms of invention were strikingly similar to simplified registers and shared many features common to pidgin languages all over the world. The boys' language also demonstrated their stunning creativity, verbal virtuosity, performative spontaneity, and artistic improvisation. These innovative and playful processes all contributed to the creolization process they employed to expand and elaborate their language. Their inventiveness was pragmatic. They developed aspects of their language that were specifically necessary to communicate in areas of central importance in their friendship and playful interactions. They actually overlexicalize in areas of primary interest and attention, for example, in expressing a range of toilet activities and speeding actions. They developed extensive ways to express future tense, irrealis, and aspectual distinctions in order to be able to plan and enact complicated narrative pretend play dramatizations. Finally, the children use language to symbolize and represent their collective identity, strong solidarity, and courageous resistance to the dominant colonial language and culture that they chose to boldly oppose and reject. These lessons are a profound gift to us from two little boys who loved each other and played together on a remote hillside in Up-Country Kenya close to a half century ago.

EPILOGUE

At the start of this book, I claimed that Sadiki and Colin's story seemed small and simple. Instead their story was complex, nuanced, and multi-layered. Their experiences raise many profound questions causing us to rethink common assumptions about young children and about language. Their "not-so-simple" story provides provocative insights about some very big ideas concerning language origins, children's innovative language competencies, and the role of play and verbal art in language genesis. Their experiences provide compelling evidence concerning the agentive roles very young children can exercise in language and culture resistance, choice, and change.

Sadiki and Colin's language began in response to a pragmatic need the two boys had to understand each other in order to be friends and playmates in their initial hillside encounter. Their early genesis of an original simplified Swahili pidgin served that immediate function and facilitated their play activities and budding friendship. The children demonstrated their abilities to effortlessly and easily overcome their encounter with the "other" when limited language proficiencies challenged their genuine communication, meaningful interactions, and close friendship. As time went on and their close bonds and friendship deepened, even as they had learned and used other languages, they continued to expand Kisisi, its linguistic form and structure, and its social semiotic functions. It was fun. It was secret. It was theirs. It was an artistic verbal spectacle that surprised and captivated unsuspecting audiences. Their verbal creativity was on full display as it publicly declared their discursive virtuosity and their border-crossing

Kisisi (Our Language): The Story of Colin and Sadiki, First Edition. Perry Gilmore.
© 2016 Perry Gilmore. Published 2016 by John Wiley & Sons, Inc.

friendship. Their new language bonded them as much as it reflected their bonds. They created a secret language with a public function. They drew attention to their exclusive membership, letting audiences know that they were invited to witness the friendship but excluded from its membership. While they played with other children regularly, they made no attempt to ever bring anyone else into their speech community. Through their language use they carved a new, exclusive and symbolic space, a separate universe, for their controversial friendship. They forged a linguistic bond, creating their own speech community, one that resisted and rejected the dominant postcolonial regime. Their wild-tongued hegemonic defiance and social boundary-crossing transgressions disturbed and disrupted racialized and strictly segregated postcolonial spaces. Where these ruptures occurred, the children opened spaces not only for themselves but for others whom they touched and changed by their transgressive friendship. Kisisi became a form of discursive parrhesia that confronted, transcended, and in some small ways transformed the harsh and brutal colonial world they lived in, a postcolonial world that strongly rejected the very friendship they treasured and shared. In their playful way, they transformed a culture of what Wa Thiong'o identified as *fear and silence*[1] into one of *courage and voice*. Their not-so-simple tale has much to teach us about a quest for language equality and social justice – theirs then and ours now.

Although describing experiences that took place four decades ago, Colin and Sadiki's story suggests new ways of better understanding and serving today's diverse youth in the complex and dynamic sociolinguistic environments they must navigate in our multilingual and multivocal global community. The story of the brief but significant life of their language offers thought-provoking lessons for today as we search to better understand the processes of negotiating linguistic hybridity in our linguistically diverse and socially unequal world. These kinds of insights can hopefully provide significant implications for intercultural language education, policy, and planning efforts. The limited glimpses of Sadiki and Colin's language experiences demonstrate the boys' remarkable linguistic resourcefulness and social agency. But while this story celebrates the language and lives of my son Colin and his friend Sadiki, it also celebrates the language capacities of *all* children and their potential for communicative brilliance. There are similar discursive behaviors and transformative processes in every child's daily social interactions and play. The unusual extreme social and environmental circumstances that Colin and Sadiki experienced created the need for their extreme and extended language creativity. We need to more carefully consider what contexts, in and out of school, would best nurture and develop the rich and too often untapped language and communicative capacities of all children.[2] Colin and Sadiki's fluid movement within and across sharply contested linguistic and cultural borders should remind us that the unmet challenges in developing successful programs for bilingual education, English language learners, and minority language speakers are not about the children and their lacking abilities, but about our own language ideologies and the deep underlying doubt in children's language competencies that are instantiated in the foundations of our educational institutions and policies.

When I was a brand new elementary school teacher in the 1960s, my second grade class performed a modified version of Shakespeare's *A Midsummer Night's Dream* for their school play. We had so much fun and the audience delighted in the performance. Afterwards one of the experienced senior teachers offered me high praise, saying, "Perry, that was great! You get blood from a stone!" For a minute I was so flattered, but quickly I realized how disturbing her metaphor was. She was suggesting that the accomplishment was mine and not the children's. She was describing the children as inanimate, unresponsive, and lifeless. For years as an educator, I have heard similar negative conceptions about children and learning. If we look closely at our children and listen to them carefully, we would know how wrong these kinds of limited conceptions of children are. Literacy scholar and activist Yetta Goodman has long urged educators to be "kidwatchers."[3] Leading educational researchers Luis Moll and Norma Gonzalez call for us to explore and value the "funds of knowledge" all children bring to every learning situation.[4] Linguistic anthropologists, ethnographers, and researchers in the area of language socialization also carry similar efforts forward by documenting everyday talk that vividly demonstrates how children regularly display communicative competencies, language creativity, and social agency in their daily lives. This kind of research firmly confronts and debunks the negative deficit perspectives that are so pervasive in education, especially in low-income, underserved, and marginalized communities. All children have much to teach us about language, learning, and culture. We need only to pay closer attention to them.

In presenting their story, I have embedded Colin and Sadiki's narrative and the creation of their language in their immediate world, examining and exploring the context of postcolonial Kenya and the dynamics of its complex hegemonic culture. But while my focus has been on postcolonial Kenya, the children's story was not necessarily shaped by Kenya's colonial history alone. Just as this story is about all children's language abilities, it is also about all places where social injustice manifests in language use. To illustrate, I will share one particularly disturbing memory.

A few months after we arrived in Kenya, an illness prompted me to go see a doctor in Nairobi. I was happy to meet the English physician, a widow who had come to Kenya with her two children. The doctor had been highly recommended. I was sick and was reassured by her confident manner. I recall thinking that she was quite strong and courageous to come to a far away place on her own with very young children to practice medicine. In addition to the routine medical exam, questions about my symptoms and her diagnosis, she also chatted less formally, asking me about my baboon fieldwork and inquiring about how, as an American, I was enjoying being in Kenya. The conversation was superficial, friendly, and pleasant, and I was glad to be reassured that the prescription she was writing out would have me healthy again in just a few days. As our side chatting was coming to an end, she said matter of factly, "Yes, this would be a great country if it wasn't for the niggers." I was speechless. She may have noticed my shocked expression. Before I could think of how to respond, she leaned forward and looked directly at me with her eyes slightly narrowed and continued, "We should have done what you did!" I could not imagine what she could possibly mean. I asked, "What?" She answered casually, "We should have killed them all."

Her words and her sentiments were not unique. They echoed in Ngugi Wa Thiong'o's bitter and strong biting prose describing the settler colonial culture in his prison diary.

> … And, so, beyond drinking whisky and whoring each other's wives and natives … and gunning natives for pleasure in this vast happy valley the settlers produced little. No art, no literature, no culture, just the making of a little dominion marred only by niggers too many to exterminate …[5]

I never saw the doctor again, but I have recalled her words with anguish and disgust many times over the past four decades. I am still stunned by her shameless openness and brutal sense of entitlement and inhumanity. Even more painful, I am haunted by the jolting parallel she named – my own guilt and shame; my own country's violent history, built on the enslavement of one population and the attempted genocide of another. It had been easy for me to stand and judge the white settler colonial Kenyans and arrogantly hold on to my own self-righteous superiority, but her contemptuous words brought me down hard. She spoke to me knowing we both shared a common history – an intimate inhumane collusion.

While the narrative about Colin and Sadiki has focused on the context of the colonial history of postcolonial Kenya, it is crucial to remember that this story of harsh racialized injustice, bold parrhesia, and resilience could unfold on any continent, in any country, as it so often has. Makoni and Pennycook astutely note that "… most communities have been affected by colonialism and slavery at one time or another."[6] We all struggle with the aftermath of these brutal colonial histories, which surface across the globe in subtle, overt, and complex ways in today's volatile global politics, widespread social ills, and drastic and unjust power inequities. Pidgin and creole languages often mirror these harsh inequities and master/slave relationships.

Martin Calder wrote, "The confrontation with the unknown in language inevitably produces a reassessment of the known. Stories of the encounter with the other have written into them stories of the discovery, and rediscovery, of the self."[7] The British doctor harshly reminds us to turn the spotlight back on ourselves when examining the other. So, too, David Smith echoes this lesson when he writes, "The real challenge is not to understand [society] but to understand ourselves and why we have created it the way it is."[8] Hopefully, the story of Colin and Sadiki will linger in your memory as another lesson in humanity, inspiring you to further question, wonder, and explore conceptions of our own irrepressible human language creativity and the quest for a more just and aggressive pursuit of language equality in our global education, policy, and planning practices.

IN MEMORIAM

Colin Gilmore

September 10, 1969 – May 13, 1988

NOTES

Prologue

1   Language ecology, or ecolinguistics, refers to the study of interactions between languages and their environments, i.e., natural, social, psychological, and political. See Haugen (1972), Mufwene (2001), Skutnabb-Kangas (2011)
2   Fabian (2008: viii)

Chapter 1

1   Calder (2003: 13)
2   Merton (1968: 157–158)
3   Gilmore (1977)
4   Wolfe (1968)
5   Le Breton (1968), Vitale (1980)
6   Polomé (1971)
7   Hancock (1971: 519)
8   Piaget (1926)
9   Gilmore (1983a)
10   Slobin (1997)
11   Schieffelin (1990)
12   Vygotsky (1978)
13   Shatz and Gelman (1977)
14   Ochs Keenan (1977)
15   Campa (2008), Remer (1965), http://en.wikipedia.org/wiki/Serendipity
16   Merton (1968), Merton and Barber (2004), Peirce (1998)
17   Hymes (1964)

Kisisi (Our Language): The Story of Colin and Sadiki, First Edition. Perry Gilmore
© 2016 Perry Gilmore. Published 2016 by John Wiley & Sons, Inc.

18 Blommaert (2013)
19 Gumperz (1965)
20 Mutonya and Parsons (2004); see also Vitale (1980) for further examples and descriptions of these Kiswahili variations

Chapter 2

1   Horatio Hale (1886) as quoted in Jespersen (1964: 181)
2   Strum (1975: 691)
3   Piaget (1926)
4   Calder (2003)
5   Herodotus (1966), Rymer (1994), Shattuck (1980)
6   Bickerton (2008), Shattuck (1980)
7   Campbell and Grieve (1982)
8   Fromkin et al. (1974), Newton (2002)
9   See for example Newton (2002) and Masson (1996)
10 Itard (1962)
11 Rymer (1994)
12 Calder (2003), Rymer (1994), Shattuck (1980)
13 Bickerton (2008)
14 Berreby (1992: 36)
15 Bickerton (2008: 126)
16 Bickerton (2008:127), see also Banks (2008)
17 Berreby (1992)
18 Bickerton (2008)
19 Higgins (2009)
20 Kegl, Senghas and Coppola (1999), Kegl (2008)
21 Bickerton (2008: 232)
22 Kettlewell (2004)
23 See Feldman, Goldin-Meadow and Gleitman (1977), Goldin-Meadow (2003) for further discussions of home sign invention
24 O'Shannessy (2013)
25 Hale (1886)
26 Jespersen (1964: 184)
27 Jespersen (1964: 185–186)
28 Horowitz (1978)
29 Forbes Magazine (2005): www.forbes.com/2005/10/19/chomsky-noam-language-invention-comm05-cx_de_1024chomskyinvent.html
30 For further examples and discussions of idioglossia and twin language, see Bakker (1987), Hale (1886), Horowitz (1978), Jespersen (1964), Luria and Yudovitch (1956)
31 Gilmore (1979a)
32 Samarin personal correspondence November 2, 1981
33 Samarin (1967)

34   Samarin (1963)

35   Samarin (1971)

36   Harding, personal correspondence November 20, 2013

37   Bucholtz (1999)

38   Gilmore (1979a), Gilmore (1981), Gilmore (2008a), Gilmore (2009), Gilmore (2011b)

39   For example debates about language versus dialect, see also Makoni and Pennycook (2007)

40   See for example DeGraff (2005), Holm (2000), Hymes (1971), Kouwenberg and Singler (2006), McWhorter (1998), McWhorter (2013), Parkvall (2000), Romaine (1988), Smith (1973), Todd (1990)

41   Parkvall (n.d.)

42   Hymes (1971: 5)

43   Todd (1990)

44   Parkvall (2000)

45   Bellugi and Brown (1971), Slobin (1997), Smith (1972)

46   Newport et al. (1975)

47   Ferguson (1971), Goldin-Meadow (2002), Jakobson (1968)

48   Schumann (1975)

49   Ferguson (1971)

50   Labov (1971), Parkvall (n.d.), Sankoff and Laberge (1980), Stewart (2007)

51   Hymes (1971); also see Mufwene (2008) for a recent and controversial counter-argument

52   Smith (1973: 290)

53   See DeGraff (2001)

54   Hymes (1971)

55   Hymes (1971: 7)

56   Smith (1973: 290)

57   Jourdan (2008: 377)

58   Hymes (1971)

59   Hymes (1971)

60   Errington (2001), Errington (2008)

61   See for example University of Bremen, International Conference on Colonial and Postcolonial Linguistics. September 2013: www.cpl.uni-bremen.de

62   Pratt (1991: 34)

63   Hymes (1971: 5)

64   For discussions and critiques of the concept of speech community, see Blommaert (2007), Gumperz (1965), Hymes (1968), Hymes (1992), Mendoza-Denton (2011), Morgan (2004), Morgan (2014)

65   DeGraff (1999: 488), see also Seigel (2006)

66   Gicheru and Gachuhu (1984: 11)

67   Gicheru and Gachuhu (1984: 11)

68   Gichru and Gachuhi (1984), Githinji (2006), Kiefling and Mous (2004), Mazrui (1995), Spyropoulos (1987)

69 Halliday (1976), Githiora (2002), Ogechi (2005)
70 Bosire (2006), Kang'ethe-Iraki (2004), Mazrui (1995), Orcutt-Gachiri (2011), Rudd (2008), Samper (2002)
71 Orcutt-Gachiri (2011)
72 Mazuri (1995: 444)
73 Bosire (2006: 192)
74 Rudd (2008: 162)
75 Samper (2002: vii)
76 Samper (2002: 2)
77 Bakhtin (1981)
78 Bhabba (1984)
79 Samper (2002: 11–12)
80 Samper (2002: 148)
81 Halliday (1976)
82 Sapir (1949)

Chapter 3

1 Callois (1961: 13)
2 Huizinga (1955: 28)
3 Gilmore (1979a)
4 Jakobson (1971)
5 See for example Bauman (1982), Kirshenblatt-Gimblett (1976), Opie and Opie (2001)
6 Chukovsky (1963)
7 Chukovsky (1963: 1)
8 Bauman (1982: 173)
9 Bauman (1982)
10 Gilmore and Smith (1982), Gilmore and Glatthorn (1982), Gilmore (1983a), Gilmore (1983b), Gilmore (1985), Gilmore (1986)
11 Jourdan (2008)
12 Jakobson (1971)
13 Cazden (1972), Garvey (1977), Sanchez and Kirshenblatt-Gimblett (1976)
14 Garvey (1977)
15 Hymes (1964), Sanchez and Kirshenblatt-Gimblett (1976)
16 Strum (1975)
17 Samarin, personal communication, November 2, 1981
18 Garvey (1977), Jakobson (1971), Jespersen (1964)
19 Ochs Keenan (1977)
20 Sutton-Smith (1976)
21 Ochs Keenan (1977)
22 Cremin and Maybin (2013: 279)
23 Chukovsky (1963: 103)
24 Shatz and Gelman (1977)

25 Jakobson (1968)
26 Sanchez and Kirshenblatt-Gimblett (1976)
27 Halliday (1976: 578)
28 Feldman, Goldin-Meadow, and Gleitman (1977)
29 For further discussion see Gleitman and Newport (1995)
30 Kettlewell (2004)
31 Kirshenblatt-Gimblett (1976), Sherzer (1976)
32 Whinnom (1971)
33 Mukarovsky (1970)
34 Cremin and Maybin (2013: 275)
35 Hymes (1973), Philips (2007)
36 www.itvs.org/video/last-white-man-standing-video-extra
37 Bourdieu (1977)
38 Foucault (2001), Gilmore (2008b)
39 Goffman (1956), Goffman (1963)
40 Jaffe (2009: 3)
41 Blommaert (2007: 203), Goffman (1963)
42 Goffman (1963), Goffman (1955)
43 Silverstein (1993)
44 Bucholtz (1999: 12)
45 See Hornberger and Johnson (2007), McCarty (2011)
46 Schieffelin (2002: 156)
47 Woolard (1998)
48 Lévi-Strauss (1962)
49 Vergès (2003), as quoted in Knepper (2006: 71)
50 Hirsch (2002: xii)
51 Maurer (1998: viii), Lorca (1998)
52 Maurer (1998: 62)
53 Maurer (1998: 56)
54 Maurer (1998: 58)
55 Hirsch (2002)
56 Maurer (1998)

Chapter 4

1 Jourdan (2008: 360)
2 Wolfe (2006: 388)
3 Haraway (1989b: 296)
4 Morgan (1963)
5 Ndege (2009)
6 Morgan (1963), Frontani and Hewitt (2006)
7 Maxon (2001)
8 Frontani and Hewitt (2006: 15)
9 Ndege (2009), Wa Thiong'o (1981), Zeleza (1992)

10 Wolfe (2006)
11 Bob Harding, personal communication, November 20, 2013
12 Riley (2003: 183)
13 Riley (2003), Frontani and Hewitt (2006), Cole (1975)
14 Strum (1987: 206)
15 Frontani and Hewitt (2006: 32)
16 www.itvs.org/films/last-white-man-standing
17 www.itvs.org/films/last-white-man-standing
18 Cole (1975: 34)
19 Williams (1977)
20 Rifkin (2013: 336)
21 Frontani and Hewitt (2006: 32)
22 Rifkin (2013: 337)
23 Maxon (2001: 38)
24 Maxon (2001: 38)
25 Maxon (2001: 38)
26 Wa Thiong'o (1981), see also Grinker et al. (2010)
27 Wa Thiong'o (1981: 36–37)
28 Wa Thiong'o (1981)
29 Wa Thiong'o (1981: 37)
30 Wa Thiong'o (1981: 37)
31 Wa Thiong'o (1981: 36)
32 Wa Thiong'o (1981: 35)
33 Wa Thiong'o (1981: 38)
34 Wa Thiong'o (1981: 38)
35 Cole (1975: 65)
36 Cole (1975: 32)
37 Strum (1987)
38 For further details see Strum (1987)
39 For further details see www.google.com/#q=baboons+r+us
40 Coniff (2007), Frontani and Hewitt (2006), McIntosh (forthcoming b), Wa Thiong'o (1981), and Strum personal communication, January 3, 2015
41 Haraway (1989a), Haraway (1989b)
42 Wa Thiong'o (1981: 31)
43 Haraway (1989a: 296)
44 Haraway (1989a: 296)
45 Strum (1987: 205)
46 McIntosh (forthcoming a)
47 Lessing (1950)
48 Strum (1987: 17)
49 Conniff (2007: 40)
50 Conniff (2007), McIntosh (2009), McIntosh (2010), Nicholls (2005)
51 http://en.wikipedia.org/wiki/Settler_Swahili
52 Le Breton (1968: 1)

53 Le Breton (1968: 39)
54 Le Breton (1968: 44)
55 Le Breton (1968: 51)
56 Hill (1980: 96)
57 Gilmore (2011)
58 Myers-Scotton (1978: 723)
59 Myers-Scotton (1978: 724)
60 Myers-Scotton (1978: 733)
61 Myers-Scotton (1978: 733)
62 Bakhtin (1981)
63 Foucault (1972)
64 Zweig (2004)
65 Denis (1988), http://web.cocc.edu/cagatucci/classes/hum211/CoursePack/Chocolat.htm
66 www.itvs.org/films/last-white-man-standing
67 Barnes (2013)
68 http://mobile.nation.co.ke/lifestyle/Happy-Valley-Death-Books-History-Kenya/-/1950774/2206942/-/format/xhtml/-/12jguefz/-/index.html
69 Hill (1993)
70 Schieffelin, Woolard and Kroskrity (1999), Gonzalez (2001)
71 Ochs and Schieffelin (1986)
72 Hornberger and Johnson (2007), Johnson (2009), McCarty (2011)
73 Gilmore (1979a), Gilmore (1979b), Gilmore (1983a)
74 Pennycook (1998)
75 Gonzalez (2001: xxii)
76 Makihara and Schieffelin (2007: 16)
77 Ochs (2009: 545)
78 Wa Thiong'o (1981)
79 McIntosh (forthcoming b)
80 Conniff (2007: 40)
81 http://www.itvs.org/films/last-white-man-standing
82 McIntosh (forthcoming b: 11)
83 Crowley and Hawhee (2004)
84 Foucault (2001: 5)
85 Foucault (2001: 6)
86 Gilmore (2008b)
87 Gilmore (2008b)
88 Wa Thiong'o (1981)
89 Anzaldua (1987)

Chapter 5

1 Bell (2014: 77)
2 Makoni and Pennycook (2007: 1)

3 Bauman and Briggs (2003)
4 Irvine and Gal (2000: 47)
5 Makoni and Pennycook (2007: 4)
6 DeGraff (2005)
7 DeGraff (2005: 534)
8 Makoni and Pennycook (2007: 20)
9 Makoni and Pennycook (2007: 20–21)
10 Samarin (1971)
11 Le Breton (1968: 7); for a current Swahili pronunciation guide see http://kamusi.org/content/swahili-pronunciation-guide
12 Sankoff and Laberg (1973)
13 Halliday (1976: 571)
14 Halliday (1976: 571)
15 DeCamp (1971)
16 Bickerton (1975)
17 Slobin (1997)
18 Comrie (1976: 5)
19 Wald (1973)
20 Wald (1973), Heine (1973), Polomé (1972)
21 Bosire (2006), Kang'ethe-Iraki (2004), Mazrui (1995), Rudd (2008), Samper (2002)
22 Comrie (1976: 41)
23 Comrie (1976: 42)
24 Wald (1973)
25 Wald (1973: 131)
26 Bickerton (1975)
27 Bickerton (1975: 59)
28 Bickerton (1975)
29 Aston (1944), cited in Wald (1973)
30 See Wald (1973: 117) for further discussion
31 Gilmore (2011b)
32 Parkvall, personal communication, November 10, 2010

EPILOGUE

1 Wa Thiong'o (1981)
2 See for example Gilmore and Glatthorn (1982), Gilmore and Smith (1982), Gilmore (1983b), Gilmore (1985), Hymes (1972), Smith (1983)
3 Goodman (1985)
4 Gonzalez, Moll, and Amanti (2005)
5 Wa Thiong'o (1981: 30)
6 Makoni and Pennycook (2007: 20)
7 Calder (2003: 13)
8 Smith (2002: 182–183)

REFERENCES

Anzaldua, G. (1987) *Borderlands/La Frontera: The New Mestiza*. San Francisco: Spinsters/Aunt Lute.

Bakhtin, M. (1981) *The Dialogic Imagination: Four Essays* (translated by M. Holquist and C. Emerson). Austin: University of Texas Press.

Bakker, P. (1987) Autonomous Language of Twins. *Acta Geneticae Medicae et Gemellologiae (Roma)*, 36(2): 233–238.

Banks, E. (2008) Return to Fantasy Island: An Embattled Scholar Still Champions His Dream Experiment in Language Formation. *Chronicle of Higher Education*, 58(37). http://listserv.linguistlist.org/pipermail/lgpolicy-list/2008-May/007182.html

Barnes, J. (2013) *The Ghosts of Happy Valley: Searching for the Lost World of Africa's Infamous Aristocrats*. London: Aurum Press.

Bauman, R. (1982) The Ethnography of Children's Folklore. In: P. Gilmore and A. Glatthorn (eds) *Children In and Out of School: Ethnography and Education*. Washington, DC: Center for Applied Linguistics, pp. 172–187.

Bauman, R. and C. Briggs (2003) *Voices of Modernity: Language Ideologies and the Politics of Inequality*. New York: Cambridge University Press.

Bell, A. (2014) *The Guidebook to Sociolinguistics*. Malden, MA: Wiley Blackwell.

Bellugi, U. and R. Brown (eds) (1971) *The Acquisition of Language*. Chicago: University of Chicago Press.

Berreby, D. (1992) Kids, Creoles, and the Coconuts. *Discovery Magazine*, April: 42–53.

Bhabba, H. (1994) *The Location of Culture*. New York: Routledge.

Bickerton, D. (1975) *Dynamics of a Creole System*. Cambridge: Cambridge University Press.

Bickerton, D. (2008) *Bastard Tongues*. New York: Hill and Wang.

Blommaert, J. (2007) *Discourse: Key Topics in Sociolinguistics*. New York: Cambridge University Press.

Blommaert, J. (2013) *Ethnography, Superdiversity and Linguistic Landscapes: Chronicles of Complexity*. Bristol: Multilingual Matters.

Bosire, M. (2006) Hybrid Languages: The Case of Sheng. In: O. Arasanyin and M. Pemberton (eds) *Selected Proceedings of the 36th Annual Conference on African Linguistics*. Somerville: Cascadilla Proceedings Project, pp. 185–193.

Bourdieu, P. (1977) The Economics of Linguistic Exchanges. *Social Science Information*, 16: 645–668.

Bucholtz, M. (1999) Bad Examples: Transgression and Progress in Language and Gender Studies. In: M. Bucholtz, A.C. Lang and L. Sutton (eds) *Reinventing Identities*. New York: Oxford University Press, pp. 3–24.

Calder, M. (2003) *Encounters with the Other: A Journey to the Limits of Language through Works by Rousseau, Defoe, Prévost and Graffignuy*. Amsterdam: Rodolpi.

Callois, R. (1961) *Man, Play and Games*. Chicago: University of Illinois.

Campa, R. (2008) Making Science by Serendipity. A Review of Robert K. Merton and Elinor Barber's *The Travels and Adventures of Serendipity*. *Journal of Evolution and Technology*, 17(1): 75–83.

Campbell, R.N. and R. Grieve (1982) Royal Investigations of the Origin of Language. *Historiographia Linguistica*, 9(1–2): 43–74.

Cazden, C. (1972) *Child Language and Education*. New York: Holt, Rinehart and Winston.

Chukovsky, K. (1963) *From Two to Five* (translated and edited by Miriam Morton). Berkeley: University of California Press.

Cole, E. (1975) *Random Recollections of a Pioneer Kenya Settler*. Woodbridge, Suffolk: Baron.

Comrie, B. (1976) *Aspect*. Cambridge: Cambridge University Press.

Conniff, R. (2007) Death in Happy Valley. *Smithsonian*, February: 40–53.

Cremin, T. and J. Maybin (2013) Children's and Teacher's Creativity In and Through Language. In: K. Hall, T. Cremin, B. Comber and L. Moll (eds) *International Handbook of Research on Children's Literacy, Learning and Culture*. Malden: Wiley-Blackwell, pp. 275–290.

Crowley, S. and D. Hawhee (2004) *Ancient Rhetorics for Contemporary Students*. Upper Saddle River, New Jersey: Pearson.

De Camp, D. (1971) Toward a Generative Analysis of a Post-Creole Speech Continuum. In: D. Hymes (ed.) *Pidginization and Creolization of Languages*. New York: Cambridge University Press.

DeGraff, M. (1999) Creolization, Language Change and Language Acquisition. An Epilogue. In: M. DeGraff (ed.) *Language Creation and Language Change: Creolization, Diachrony, and Development*. Cambridge: MIT Press, pp. 473–543.

DeGraff, M. (2005) Linguists' Most Dangerous Myth: The Fallacy of Creole Exceptionalism. *Language in Society*, 34: 533–591.

Denis, C. (1988) *Chocolat* (film). France: Orion Classics.

Errington, J. (2001) Colonial Linguistics. *Annual Review of Anthropology*, 30: 19–39.

Errington, J. (2008) *Linguistics in a Colonial World: A Story of Language, Meaning, and Power.* Boston: Wiley-Blackwell.

Fabian, J. (2008) *Ethnography as Commentary: Writing from the Virtual Archive.* Durham: Duke University Press.

Feldman, H., S. Goldin-Meadow, and L. Gleitman (1977) Beyond Herodotus: The Creation of Language by Linguistically Deprived Deaf Children. In: A. Lock (ed.) *Action, Gesture and Symbol: The Emergence of Language.* New York: Academic Press, pp. 351–414.

Ferguson, C. (1971) *Language Structure and Language Use: Essays by Charles Ferguson.* Stanford: Stanford University Press.

Foucault, M. (1972) *Power and Knowledge.* New York: Pantheon Books.

Foucault, M. (2001) *Fearless Speech* (edited by J. Pearson). Los Angeles: Semio-text(e).

Fromkin, V., S. Krashen, S. Curtiss, D. Rigler and M. Rigler (1974) The Development of Language in Genie: A Case of Language Acquisition beyond the "Critical Period". *Brain and Language*, 1: 81–107.

Frontani, H. and R. Hewitt (2006) Ideologies of Land and Place: Gikuyu and Settler Colonist Women in Kenya. *Geographical Bulletin*, 47: 14–35.

Garvey, C. (1977) *Play.* Cambridge: Harvard University Press.

Gicheri, C. and R. Gachuhu (1984) Sheng: New Language Baffles Parents. *Daily Nation,* March 14. Nairobi, Kenya.

Gilmore, H. (2011) Taught to the Tune of the Hickory Stick: Swahili Simplified. http://www.chestnuthilllocal.com/blog/2011/04/21/taught-to-the-tune-of-a-hickory-stick-swahili-simplified/

Gilmore, P. (1977) Juvenile Social Learning: The Role of Infant Retrievals. Unpublished Masters paper, Temple University.

Gilmore, P. (1979a) A Children's Pidgin: The Case of a Spontaneous Pidgin for Two. *Working Papers in Sociolinguistics*, 64: 15–38.

Gilmore, P. (1979b) Micro-macro Analysis of a Children's Pidgin. Paper presented at the Committee on Cognitive and Linguistic Studies, 78th Annual Meeting of the American Anthropological Association, Cincinnati, Ohio, November 28– December 2.

Gilmore, P. (1981) Tense and Aspect in a Children's Pidgin. Unpublished manuscript, University of Pennsylvania.

Gilmore, P. (1983a) Ethnographic Approaches to Child Language. *Volta Review* 85: 234–255.

Gilmore, P. (1983b) Spelling Mississippi: Recontextualizing a Literacy Related Speech Event. *Anthropology and Education Quarterly*, 14(4): 234–255.

Gilmore, P. (1985) Gimme Room: School Resistance, Attitude and Access to Literacy. *Journal of Education*, 167:111–128.

Gilmore, P. (1986) Sub-Rosa Literacy: Peers, Play and Ownership in Literacy. In: B. Schieffelin and P. Gilmore (eds) *The Acquisition of Literacy: EthnographicPerspectives.* Norwood, New Jersey: Ablex, pp. 155–170.

Gilmore, P. (2008a) *Creating and Recreating Language Communities: Verbal Practices Transform Social Structure and Reconstruct Identities on a Kenya Hillside and in the Alaska Interior.* Paper presented at the Sociolinguistic Symposium, Amsterdam, April 17.

Gilmore, P. (2008b) Engagement on the Backroads: Insights for Anthropology and Education. *Anthropology and Education Quarterly*, 39(2): 109–116.

Gilmore, P. (2009) Our Language. In: R.A. Shweder (ed.) *The Child: An Encyclopedic Companion.* Chicago: University of Chicago Press, pp. 546–547.

Gilmore, P. (2011a) Language Ideologies, Ethnography and Ethnology: New Directions in Anthropological Approaches to Language Policy. In: T. McCarty (ed.) *Ethnography and Language Policy.* New York: Routledge, pp. 121–127.

Gilmore, P. (2011b) We Call It "Our Language": A Children's Swahili Pidgin Transforms Social and Symbolic Order on a Remote Hillside in Up-Country Kenya. *Anthropology and Education Quarterly*, 42(4): 370–392.

Gilmore, P. and A. Glatthorn (eds) (1982) *Children In and Out of School: Ethnography and Education.* Washington, DC: Center for Applied Linguistics.

Gilmore, P. and D.M. Smith (1982) A Retrospective Discussion of the State of the Art of Ethnography and Education. In: P. Gilmore and A. Glatthorn (eds) *Children In and Out of School: Ethnography and Education.* Washington, DC: Center for Applied Linguistics.

Githinji, P. (2006) Bazes and Their Shibboleths: Lexical Variation and Sheng Speakers' Identity in Nairobi. *Nordic Journal of African Studies* 15(4):443–472.

Githiora, C. (2002) Sheng: Peer Language, Swahili Dialect or Emerging Creole? *Journal of African Cultural Studies*, 15(2): 159–181.

Gleitman, L.R. and E.L. Newport (1995) The Invention of Language by Children: Environmental and Biological Influences on the Acquisition of Language. In: L.R. Gleitman and M. Liberman (eds) *Language: An Invitation to Cognitive Science.* Cambridge: MIT Press, pp. 1–24.

Goffman, E. (1956) *The Presentation of Self In Everyday Life.* New York: Anchor.

Goffman, E. (1963) *Behavior in Public Places.* New York: Free Press.

Goldin-Meadow, S. (2002) Getting a Handle on Language Creation. In: T. Givon and B. Malle (eds) *The Evolution of Language out of Pre-Language.* Philadelphia: Johns Benjamins, pp. 343–374.

Goldin-Meadow, S. (2003) *The Resilience of Language: What Gesture Creation in Deaf Children Can Tell Us About How All Children Learn Language.* New York: Psychology Press.

Gonzalez, N. (2001) *I Am My Language.* Tucson: University of Arizona Press.

Gonzalez, N., L. Moll and C. Amanti (2005) *Funds of Knowledge: Theorizing Practices in Households, Communities and Classrooms.* New York: Routledge.

Goodman, Y.M. (1985) Kidwatching: Observing Children in the Classroom. In: A. Jagger and M.T. Smith-Burke (eds) *Observing the Language Learner.* Urbana: NCTE and IRA, pp. 9–18.

Grinker, R., S. Lubkemann and C. Steiner (eds) (2010) *Perspectives on Africa: A Reader in Culture, History and Representation.* Malden: Wiley-Blackwell.

Gumperz, J. (1965) The Speech Community. *Encyclopedia of the Social Sciences*, 9(3): 382–386.

Hale, H. (1886) The Origin of Languages and the Antiquity of Speaking Man. *American Association for the Advancement of Science*, xv.

Halliday, M.A.K. (1976) Anti-Languages. *American Anthropologist*, 78(3): 570–584.

Hancock, I. (1971) A Survey of the Pidgins and Creoles of the World. In: D.H. Hymes (ed.) *Pidginization and Creolization of Languages*. New York: Cambridge University Press, pp. 509–523.

Haraway, D. (1989a) Monkeys, Aliens, and Women: Love, Science, and Politics at The Intersection of Feminist Theory and Colonial Discourse. *Woman's Studies International Forum*, 12(3): 295–312.

Haraway, D. (1989b) *Primate Visions*. New York: Routledge.

Haugen, E. (1972) *The Ecology of Language*. Stanford: Stanford University Press.

Heine, B. (1973) Zur Genetischen Gliederung Der Bantu-Sprachen. *Afrika und Übersee*, 56(3): 164–185.

Herodotus (and A. de Selincourt) (1966) *The Histories, Book II*. Harmondsworth: Penguin Classics.

Higgins, C. (2009) *English as a Local Language: Post-colonial Identities and Multilingual Practices*. Bristol: Multilingual Matters.

Hill, A. (1980) Zinjanthropus: An Uncertain je ne sais quoi. *New Scientist*, January 10: 96.

Hill, J. (1993) Hasta La Vista Baby: Anglo Spanish in the American Southwest. *Critique of Anthropology*, 13(2): 145–176.

Hirsch, E. (2002) *The Demon and the Angel: Searching for the Source of Artistic Inspiration*. New York: Harcourt.

Holm, J. (2000) *An Introduction to Pidgins and Creoles*. New York: Cambridge University Press.

Hornberger, N. and D.C. Johnson (2007) Slicing the Onion Ethnographically: Layers and Spaces in Multilingual Language Education Policy and Practice. *TESOL Quarterly* 41(3): 509–532.

Horowitz, J. (1978) Breaking the Code That Binds. *Los Angeles Times*, April 2 (1): 20–23.

Huizinga, J. (1955) *Homo Ludens*. Boston: Beacon Press.

Hymes, D.H. (1964) Introduction: Toward Ethnographies of Communication. *American Anthropologist*, 66(6): 1–34.

Hymes, D.H. (1968) The Ethnography of Speaking. In: J. Fishman (ed.) *Readings in the Sociology of Language*. The Hague: Mouton, pp. 99–138.

Hymes, D.H. (1971) Preface. In: D.H. Hymes (ed.) *Pidginization and Creolization of Languages*. New York: Cambridge University Press, pp. 3–11.

Hymes, D.H. (1972) Introduction. In: C. Cazden, V. John and D. Hymes (eds) *Functions of Language in the Classroom*. New York: Teachers College Press, pp. xi–lvii.

Hymes, D.H. (1973) Speech and Language: On the Origins and Foundations of Inequality among Speakers. *Daedalus*, 102(3): 59–85.

Hymes, D.H. (1992) The Concept of Communicative Competence Revisited. In: M. Putz (ed.) *Thirty Years of Linguistic Evolution*. Philadelphia: Johns Benjamins, pp. 31–57.

Irvine, J.T. and S. Gal (2000) Language Ideology and Linguistic Differentiation. In: P.V. Kroskrity (ed.) *Regimes of Language: Ideologies, Politics, and Identities*. Santa Fe: School of American Research Press, pp. 35–84.

Itard, J. (1962) *The Wild Boy of Aveyron*. New York: Appleton-Century-Crofts.

Jaffe, A. (2009) Introduction. In: A. Jaffe (ed.) *Stance: Sociolinguistic Perspectives*. New York: Oxford University Press, pp. 3–28.

Jakobson, R. (1968) Poetry of Grammar and Grammar of Poetry. *Lingua* 21: 597–609.

Jakobson, R. (1971) *Studies on Child Language and Aphasia*. The Hague: Mouton.

Jespersen, O. (1964) *Language: Its Nature, Development and Origin*. New York: Norton.

Johnson, D.C. (2009) Ethnography of Language Policy. *Language Policy*, 8: 139–159.

Jourdan, C. (2008) The Culture in Pidgin Genesis. In: S. Kouwenberg and J.V. Singler (eds) *The Handbook of Pidgin and Creole Studies*. Malden: Blackwell, pp. 359–382.

Kang'ethe-Iraki, F. (2004) Cognitive Efficiency: The Sheng Phenomenon in Kenya. *Pragmatics*, 14(1): 55–68.

Kegl, J. (2008) The Case of Signed Languages in the Context of Pidgin and Creole Studies. In: S. Kouwenberg and J.V. Singler (eds) *The Handbook of Pidgin and Creole Studies*. Malden: Blackwell, pp. 491–511.

Kegl. J., A. Senhas and M.V. Coppola (1999) Creation Through Contact: Sign Language Emergence and Sign Language Change in Nicaragua. In: M. DeGraff (ed.) *Language Creation and Language Change*. Cambridge: Cambridge University Press, pp. 179–237.

Kettlewell, J. (2004) Children create new sign language. BBC News Online. http://news.bbc.co.uk/2/hi/science/nature/3662928.stm

Kiefling, R. and M. Mous (2004) Urban Youth Languages in Africa. *Anthropological Linguistics*, 46(3): 303–341.

Kirshenblatt-Gimblett, B. (1976) *Speech Play: Research and Resources for Studying Linguistic Creativity*. Philadelphia: University of Pennsylvania Press, 1976.

Knepper, W. (2006) Colonization, Creolization, and Globalization: The Art and Ruses of Bricolage. *Small Axe*, 21(10): 70–86.

Kouwenberg, S. and J.V. Singler (eds) (2008) *The Handbook of Pidgin and Creole Studies*. Malden: Blackwell.

Labov, W. (1971) The Notion of 'System' in Creole Languages. In: D.H. Hymes (ed.) *Pidginization and Creolization of Languages*. New York: Cambridge University Press, pp. 447–472.

Le Breton, F.H. (1968) *Up-Country Swahili*. Surrey, England: R.W. Simpson.

Lessing, D. (1950) *The Grass is Singing*. London: Thomas Y. Crowell Company.

Levi-Straus, C. (1962) *The Savage Mind*. Chicago: University of Chicago Press.

Lorca, F. (1998) Theory and Play of the Duende. In: *In Search of Duende* (edited by Christopher Maurer). New York: New Directions, pp. 56–72.

Luria, R.A. and F. Ia.Yudovitch (1956) *Speech and the Development of Mental Process in the Child*. London: Staple Press.

Makoni, S. and A. Pennycook (2007) *Disinventing and Reconstituting Languages*. Bristol: Multilingual Matters.

Makihara, M. and B. Schieffelin (eds) (2007) *Consequences of Contact: Language Ideologies and Social Transformations in Pacific Societies*. New York: Oxford University Press.

Masson, J.M. (1996) *The Wild Child: The Unsoved Mystery of Kasper Hauser*. New York: Free Press Paperbacks.

Maurer, C. (ed.) (1998) *In Search of Duende*. New York: New Directions.

Maxon, R.M. (2001) *Struggle for Kenya: The Loss and Reassertion of Imperial Initiative, 1912–1923*. Madison, New Jersey: Fairleigh Dickinson University Press.

Mazrui, A. (1995) Slang and Codeswitching: The Case of Sheng in Kenya. *Afrikanistische Arbeitspapiere*, 42: 168–179.

McCarty, T. (ed.) (2011) *The Ethnography of Language Policy*. New York: Routledge.

McIntosh, J. (2009) Stance and Distance: Social Boundaries, Self-Lamination, and Metalinguistic Anxiety in White Kenyan Narratives about the African Occult. In: A. Jaffe (ed.) *Stance: Sociolinguistic Perspectives*. New York: Oxford University Press, pp. 72–91.

McIntosh, J. (2010) *Seeing Themselves Being Seen: The Cholmondeley Case and White Kenyan Nationalism*. Invited Lecture, Stanford University Department of Anthropology, April 27, 2009.

McIntosh, J. (forthcoming a) Autochthony and "Family": The Politics of Kinship in White Kenyan Bids to Belong. *Anthopology Quarterly*. In review.

McIntosh, J. (forthcoming b) Linguistic Atonement: Penitence in White Kenyan Language Ideologies. *Anthropology Quarterly*. In review.

McWhorter, J. (1998) Identifying the Creole Prototype: Vindicating a Typological Class. *Language*, 74(4): 788–818.

McWhorter, J. (2013) *What Language Is (And What It Isn't and What It Could Be)*. New York: Penguin.

Mendoza-Denton, N. (2011) Individuals and Communities. In: B. Johnstone, R. Wodak and P. Kerswill (eds) *The Sage Handbook of Sociolinguistics*. London: Sage Publications, pp. 181–191.

Merton, R.K. (1968) *Social Theory and Social Structure*. New York: The Free Press.

Merton, R.K. and E. Barber (2004) *The Travels and Adventures of Serendipity: A Study in Sociological Semantics and the Sociology of Science*. Princeton: Princeton University Press

Morgan, M. (2004) Speech Community. In: A. Duranti (ed.) *A Companion to Linguistic Anthropology*. Malden: Blackwell, pp. 3–22.

Morgan, M. (2014) *Speech Communities*. Cambridge: Cambridge University Press.

Morgan, W.T. W. (1963) The 'White Highlands' of Kenya. *Geographical Journal,* 129(2): 140–155.

Mufwene, S. (2001) *The Ecology of Language Evolution.* Cambridge: Cambridge University Press.

Mufwene, S. (2008) *Language Evolution: Contact, Competition and Change.* New York: Continuum International Publishing Group.

Mukarovsky, J. (1970) *Aesthetic Function, Norm, and Value as Social Facts* (translated by M.E. Suino). Ann Arbor: University of Michigan.

Mutonya, M. and T. Parsons (2004) KiKar: A Swahili Variety in Kenya's Colonial Army. *Journal of African Languages and Linguistics,* 25: 111–125.

Myers-Scotton, C. (1978) Language in East Africa: Linguistic Patterns and Political Ideologies. In: J.A. Fishman (ed.) *Advances in the Study of Societal Multilingualism.* The Hague: Mouton, pp. 719–760.

Ndege, P.O. (2009) *Colonialism and its Legacies in Kenya.* Fulbright-Hays Group Lecture, Moi University, Nairobi, Kenya.

Newport, E., L. Gleitman and H. Gleitman (1975) *Contributions to the Theory of Innate Ideas from Learning: A Study of Mothers' Speech and Child Language Acquisition.* Papers and Reports on Child Language Development, 10. Stanford: Stanford University Press.

Newton, M. (2002) *Savage Girls and Wild Boys: A History of Feral Children.* New York: Picador.

Nicholls, C.S. (2005) *Red Strangers: The White Tribe of Kenya.* London: Timewell Press.

Ochs, E. (2009) Language and Social Life. In: R.A. Shweder (ed.) *The Child: An Encyclopedic Companion.* Chicago: University of Chicago Press, pp. 545–549.

Ochs, E. and B. Schieffelin (1986) *Language Socialization Across Cultures.* New York: Cambridge University Press.

Ochs Keenan, E. (1977) Making It Last: Repetition in Children's Discourse. In: S.E. Tripp and C.M. Kernan (eds) *Child Discourse.* New York: Academic Press, pp. 125–138.

Ogechi, N. (2005) On Lexicalization in Sheng. *Nordic Journal of African Studies,* 14(3): 334–355.

Opie, I. and P. Opie (2001) *The Language and Lore of Schoolchildren.* New York: Review Books.

Orcutt-Gachiri, H. (2011) *Kenyan Language Ideologies, Language Endangerment, and Gikuyu(Kikuyu): How Discourses of Nationalism, Education, and Development Have Placed a Large Indigenous Language at Risk.* Dissertation, University of Arizona.

O'Shannessy, C. (2013) The Role of Multiple Sources in the Formation of an Innovative Auxiliary Category in Light Warlpiri, a New Australian Mixed Language. *Language,* 89(2): 328–353.

Parkvall, M. (2000) *Out of Africa: African Influences in Atlantic Creoles.* London: Battlebridge.

Parkvall, M. (n.d., in preparation) *Pidgin Languages.* Department of Linguistics, Stockholm University.

Peirce, C. (1998) *The Essential Peirce: Selected Philosophical Writings. Volume 2 (1893–1913)*. The Peirce Edition Project. Bloomington: Indiana University Press.

Pennycook, A. (1998) *English and the Discourses of Colonialism*. New York: Routledge.

Philips, S. (2007) Language and Social Inequality. In: A. Duranti (ed.) *A Companion to Linguistic Anthropology*. Malden: Blackwell, pp. 474–495.

Piaget, J. (1926) *The Language and Thought of the Child*. London: Kegan Paul, Trench, Trubner & Co.

Polomé, E. (1972) The Katanga (Lumumbashi) Swahili Creole. In: D. Hymes (ed.) *Pidginization and Creolization of Languages*. New York: Cambridge University Press, pp. 57–59.

Pratt, M.L. (1991) Arts of the Contact Zone. *Profession*, 91: 33–40.

Remer, T. (ed.) (1965) *Serendipity and the Three Princes, from the Peregrinaggo of 1557*. Oklahoma: University of Oklahoma Press.

Rifkin, M. (2010) Settler Common Sense. *Settler Colonial Studies*, 3(3–4): 322–340.

Riley, G. (2003) *Talking Land, Breaking Land: Women Colonizing the American West and Kenya, 1840–1940*. Albuquerque: University of New Mexico Press.

Romaine, S. (1988) *Pidgin and Creole Languages*. New York: Longman.

Rudd, P.W. (2008) *Sheng: The Mixed Language of Nairobi*. Unpublished dissertation, Ball State University.

Rymer, R. (1994) *Genie: A Scientific Tragedy*. NewYork: Perennial.

Samarin, W. (1963) *A Grammar of Sango*. The Hague: Mouton Publishers.

Samarin, W. (1967) *Field Linguistics: A Guide to Linguistic Fieldwork*. New York: Holt, Rinehart and Winston.

Samarin, W. (1971) Salient and Substantive Pidginization. In: D. Hymes (ed.) *Pidginization and Creolization of Languages*. New York: Cambridge University Press, pp. 117–140.

Samper, D.A. (2002) *Talking Sheng: The Role of a Hybrid Language in the Construction of Identity and Youth Culture in Nairobi Kenya*. Unpublished dissertation, University of Pennsylvania.

Sanchez, M. and B. Kirshenblatt-Gimblett (1976) Children's Traditional Speech Play and Child Language. In: B. Kirshenblatt-Gimblett (ed.) *Speech Play: Research and Resources for Studying Linguistic Creativity*. Philadelphia: University of Pennsylvania Press, pp. 65–110.

Sankoff, G. and S. Laberge (1980) On the Acquisition of Native Speakers by a Language. In: D. Decamp and I. Hancock (eds) *Pidgins and Creoles*. Washington, DC: Georgetown University Press, pp. 73–84.

Sapir, E. (1949) The Status of Linguistics as a Science. In: D. Mandelbaum (ed.) *Culture, Language and Personality*. Berkeley: University of California Press Culture, pp. 65–77.

Schieffelin, B. (1990) *The Give and Take of Everyday Life: Language Socialization of Kaluli Children*. New York: Cambridge University Press.

Schieffelin, B. (2002) Language and Place in Children's Worlds. *Texas Linguistic Forum* 45: 151–166.

Schieffelin, B., K. Woolard and P. Kroskrity (eds) (1999) *Language Ideologies: Practice and Theory*. New York: Oxford University Press.

Schumann, J. (1975) *Second Language Acquisition: The Pidginization Hypothesis*. Dissertation, Graduate School of Education, Harvard University.

Seigel, J. (2006) *The Emergence of Pidgin and Creole Languages*. Oxford: Oxford University Press.

Shattuck, R. (1980) *The Forbidden Experiment*. New York: Farrar, Straus and Giroux.

Shatz, M. and R. Gelman (1977) Beyond Syntax: The Influence of Conversational Constraints on Speech Modifications. In: C. Ferguson and C. Snow (eds) *Talking to Children: Input and Acquisition*. Cambridge: Cambridge University Press, pp. 189–198.

Sherzer, J. (1976) Play Languages: Implications for (Socio) Linguistics. In: B. Kirshenblatt-Gimblett (ed.) *Speech Play: Research and Resources for the Study of Linguistic Creativity*. Philadelphia: University of Pennsylvania Press, pp. 19–36.

Silverstein, M. (1993) Metapragmatic Discourse and Metapragmatic Function. In: J. Lucy (ed.) *Reflexive Language: Reported Speech and Metapragmatics*. New York: Cambridge, pp. 33–58.

Singler, J.V. (2006) Children and Creole Genesis. *Journal of Pidgin and Creole Languages* 21(1): 157–170.

Skutnabb-Kangas, T. (2011) Language Ecology. In: J. Ostman and J. Verschueren (eds) *Pragmatics in Practice*. Amsterdam: John Benjamins, pp. 177–198.

Slobin, D. (ed.) (1997) *The Crosslinguistic Study of Language Acquisition. Volume 5: Expanding the Context*. Mahwah: Lawrence Erlbaum.

Smith, D.M. (1972) Some Implications for the Social Statuses of Pidgin Languages. In: D. Smith and R. Shuy (eds) *Sociolinguistics and Cross-Cultural Analysis*. Washington, DC: Georgetown University Press, pp. 47–56.

Smith, D.M. (1973) Creolization and Language Ontogeny. In: C.J. Bailey and R. Shuy (eds) *New Ways of Analyzing Variation in English*. Washington, DC: Georgetown University Press, pp. 287–296.

Smith, D.M. (1983) Ethnographic Monitoring of Children's Acquisition of Reading/Language Arts Skills In and Out of the Classroom: General Findings. *The Generator*, Winter: 185–198.

Smith, D.M. (2002) The Challenge of Urban Ethnography. In: Y. Zou and E. Trueba (eds) *Ethnography and Schools*. Boulder: Rowman and Littlefield, pp. 171–184.

Spyropoulos, M. (1987) Sheng: Some Preliminary Investigations into a Recently Emerged Nairobi Street Language. *Journal of the Anthropological Society*, 18(1): 125–136.

Stewart, C. (ed.) (2007) *Creolization: History, Ethnography, Theory*. Walnut Creek: Left Coast Press.

Strum, S. (1975) Life with the Pumphouse Gang. *National Geographic*, 147(5): 673–691.

Strum, S. (1987) *Almost Human*. New York: Random House.

Sutton-Smith, B. (1976) A Developmental Structural Account of Riddles. In: B. Kirshenblatt-Gimblett (ed.) *Speech Play: Research and Resources for the Study of Linguistic Creativity*. Philadelphia: University of Pennsylvania Press, pp.111–120.

Todd, L. (1990) *Pidgins and Creoles*. New York: Routledge.

Vitale, A. (1980) Kesetla: Linguistic and Sociolinguistic Aspects of a Pidgin Swahili of Kenya. *Anthropological Linguistics*, 22(2): 47–65.

Vygotsky, L. (1978) *Mind in Society: The Development of Higher Psychological Processes* (edited by M. Cole, V. John-Steiner, S. Scribner, and E. Souberman). Cambridge: Harvard University Press.

Wald, B. (1973) Variation in the System of Tense Markers of Mombasa Swahili. Unpublished dissertation, Columbia University.

Wa Thiong'o, N. (1981) *Detained: A Writer's Prison Diary*. London: Heinemann.

Whinnom, K. (1971) Linguistic Hybridization and the "Special Case" of Pidgins and Creoles. In: D. Hymes (ed.) *Pidginization and Creolization of Languages*. New York: Cambridge University Press, pp. 91–115.

Williams, R. (1977) *Marxism and Literature*. New York: Oxford University Press.

Wolfe, P. (2006) Settler Colonialism and the Elimination of the Native. *Journal of Genocide Research*, 8(4): 387–409.

Wolfe, T. (1968) *The Pumphouse Gang*. New York: Farrar, Straus and Giroux.

Woolard, K.A. (1998) Language Ideology as a Field of Inquiry. In: B. Scheiffelin, K. Woolard and P. Kroskrity (eds) *Language Ideologies: Practice and Theory*. New York: Oxford University Press, pp. 3–47.

Zeleza, T. (1992) The Colonial Labour System in Kenya. In: W.R. Ochieng and R.M. Maxon (eds) *An Economic History of Kenya*. Nairobi: Heinemann East Africa, pp. 171–199.

Zweig, S. (2004) *Nowhere in Africa: An Autobiographical Novel*. Madison: Terrace Books.

INDEX

Kisisi (Our Language): The Story of Colin and Sadiki, First Edition. Perry Gilmore.
© 2016 Perry Gilmore. Published 2016 by John Wiley & Sons, Inc.

Plate 1 Proud pretend hunters look out across the savannah from high on the hillside cliff.

Plate 2 Colin and Sadiki became inseparable best friends, spending all their daylight hours together for the 15 months that they were neighbors on a remote Up-Country Kenya hillside.

Kisisi (Our Language): The Story of Colin and Sadiki, First Edition. Perry Gilmore
© 2016 Perry Gilmore. Published 2016 by John Wiley & Sons, Inc.

Plate 3 A panoramic view of the vast Kekopey ranch and flamingo-covered Lake Elementaita.

Plate 4 Colin and Sadiki look out across the savannah on a visit to Lake Elementaita where we sometimes picnicked.

Plate 5 The Red House, the Gilgil Baboon Project headquarters and our home, was frequently visited by the baboon troop who would sit on the windows and the patio and often play on the roof. For their safety, the boys had to be in the house with all the windows and doors locked when the baboons came.

Plate 6 "The Pumphouse Gang" baboons were known predators who could hunt co-operatively and take down large prey.

Plate 7 Our multilingual hillside community was made up of families who worked for the ranch and for the baboon research project. From left to right: Joab and William who worked for the baboon project, Sadiki, his father, Elim, young sister Maria, Moses (Sadiki's uncle and a worker on the ranch), a visiting relative of Moses, Mary (Moses' wife and their baby), Margaret (Sadiki's sister), Laiton (Sadiki's mother) holding baby sister Jane, and Peninah, Sadiki's older sister.

Plate 8 Sadiki's family members sometimes came from Samburu to visit. They dressed more traditionally. This beautiful aunt of Sadiki's asked me to take her picture. Her husband stands in the distant background. They had come to see the boys who loved each other so much that Mungu (God) blessed them with a language that was so complicated no one else could understand them.

Plate 9 The boys spent time together with each other's families. Sadiki's father taught the boys to make arrows and often took them with him when he went to do maintenance checks and repair at the pumphouse at the bottom of the cliff. Colin's parents took the children on short trips across the ranch to the lake or the hot springs. In this photo we are on a shopping trip in the town of Nakuru buying groceries for the month.

Plate 10 Sadiki and Colin carve arrows that Sadiki's father taught them to make.

Plate 11 A visiting entomologist they called Bwana Dudu (Mister Bug) let the boys use his insect net to collect bug specimens for which he paid them a few shillings.

Plate 12 Colin and Sadiki played long hours with Paka, Colin's adopted feral kitten. They loved to giggle and call her "Silly Paka" when she chased them and bit at their ankles.

Plate 13 Colin's father examines animal tracks with the boys.

Plate 14 Colin and Sadiki run with me through the tall grass on a picnic near Lake Elementaita.

Plate 15 Children from the Gilgil Preschool join children from the hillside at Colin's sixth birthday party. I am playing guitar and singing with the children – Sadiki's sisters and their visiting friend, Joab's twin sons, Colin and Sadiki, and their "wazungu" (white) schoolmates. This was an unusual mix since the "wazungu" children rarely interacted socially with local African children.

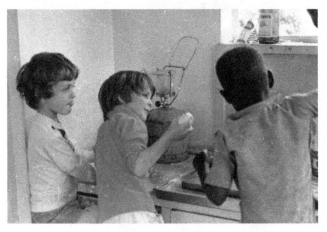

Plate 16 Colin and Sadiki often helped me make bread, shaping the flexible dough into the shapes of cars and trucks. Alan Wolf, an American friend from their preschool, joins the boys beating and shaping the dough. Alan's father was a visiting scientist studying sunbirds and their family was staying in a cottage at the Gilgil Club.

Plate 17 Colin and Sadiki take turns playing with a sling shot and a makeshift weapon they fashioned from a stick and an empty shotgun shell – one of many that could be found scattered across the landscape.

Plate 18 Sadiki and Colin look very serious as they plan a pretend hunt. They sometimes would hide in the tall grass and sneak up on a herd of Thomson's gazelles. Once they got really close they would pop up and let out shouts causing the "tommies" to scatter.

Plate 19 Sadiki and Colin loved being "silly" and enjoyed making faces for the camera.

Plate 20 Colin and Sadiki close the paddock gate.